The World and Its God

By Philip Mauro

"The Wise men are ashamed, they are dismayed and taken; lo, they have rejected the word of the Lord; and what wisdom is in them?"

(Jer. viii. 9.)

Published by Pantianos Classics

ISBN-13: 978-1717121783

First published in 1905

Contents

Publishers' Note v

Preface vi

Preface to Revised and Enlarged Edition ix

Chapter One - The Passing of Materialism . 14

Chapter Two - The Claim of The Bible 17

Chapter Three - Transformation of Life 21

Chapter Four - The World-System: Its Origin 24

Chapter Five - The Seeds of Doubt 29

Chapter Six - The Gospel of Self 33

Chapter Seven - As an Angel of Light 37

Chapter Eight - The Failure of The Scheme 43

Chapter Nine - The Bible Solution 48

Chapter Ten - "Fig Leaves" 57

Chapter Eleven - "Where Art Thou?" 62

Chapter Twelve - The Deceiver of The World 67

Chapter Thirteen - The Conditions of Faith 73

Chapter Fourteen - Divine Agencies in The World 76

Chapter Fifteen – The Way of Deliverance 80

Chapter Sixteen - The Truth About "Evolution" 84

Chapter Seventeen - Two Methods of World-Making 87

Chapter Eighteen - No Evolution Outside Human Affairs 90

Chapter Nineteen - Evolution Universal in Human Affairs 94

Chapter Twenty - No Evolution Among the Lower Animals 97

Chapter Twenty-One - Effects of Evolution 98

Chapter Twenty-Two - The Error of The Evolutionist 102

Chapter Twenty-Three - Degeneration 104

Chapter Twenty-Four - Conclusion 107

Publishers' Note

The Author of this volume, an American lawyer, was for upwards of twenty years a convinced and avowed materialist. His mental and professional training, therefore, lends lucidity and force to his arguments, which will appeal the more readily to honest minds and sincere seekers of the truth.

Preface

The purpose of this volume is to make an application of the philosophic or rationalistic test to the Bible account of Creation, and particularly to that portion of the account which deals with the Origin of Evil in human nature.

There is room just now for an application of this test, because of the collapse of the Darwinian theory of the Origin of Species. That theory, which was the central doctrine of the philosophy of Materialism, had so completely occupied the stage, that its exit leaves a most conspicuous vacancy. If evil (in its infinite variety of manifestations) be not a primal condition out of which man is evolving, and which the human race is gradually leaving behind, as Materialism taught, what is it? If we reject Materialism, as the successors of its now deceased apostles are doing, what shall take its place?

Here are patent facts—the most conspicuous matters of daily observation—viz., the distressing facts of human delinquencies and sufferings. It is not endurable that we should have no explanation of them; and Materialism, while it lasted, sufficed at least to prevent a painful void. In what direction then shall we turn to find a resting-place for our inquiring minds? In such a period of transition there will be some minds (and possibly not a few) who will be disposed to examine again (or perhaps for the first time) the explanation given by the author of Genesis, and to ascertain whether that explanation accounts for the otherwise inexplicable facts of human experience and history. To these, the following lines will afford an opportunity of making such examination, and will furnish assistance in conducting it to a sound conclusion.

Readers who are accustomed to philosophic discussions will find themselves in a familiar path so far as relates to the method employed herein; at the same time there is no attempt at profundity, and no arguments or reasonings are presented which the simple-minded and unphilosophic reader cannot readily grasp.

The volume is written from the present standpoint of one who, after having been for upwards of twenty years an implicit believer in the main doctrines of Materialism, has come to the unqualified acceptance of the first three chapters (and of all the other chapters) of Genesis, as a literal and accurate description of historic events.

The author has spoken of the passing of Materialism, and particularly of the collapse of the Darwinian theory, as the striking present-day movement of philosophic thought. It is, indeed, common to hear those who fancy themselves to be talking learnedly speak of these things as if they were still—as they were a decade ago—the almost unquestioned teachings of "science." But these (many of them, sad to say, now occupants of pulpits in Christian churches) are but merely echoing in this generation the always unproved and now properly rejected speculations of a dead and gone generation of infidel philosophers.

Preface to Revised and Enlarged Edition

In the light of criticisms and suggestions which have reached the author from various sources, it has seemed desirable to revise and amplify this work. It has been asked by several if the writer has not taken too much for granted in saying or implying that the evolutionary theories of the past generation have been generally discarded by the " Science " of to-day. There is evident need of a further word on this point in order to give a clear statement of just what the writer believes to be the truth in this connection.

A distinction is to be made between the theory of Evolution or Development, broadly (which is much older than Mr Spencer's philosophy), and the Materialism of the generation which has just passed away. The writer has spoken of the " passing of materialism" and, in particular, has called attention to the discredit which is more and more attaching to that utterly baseless conception known as the Darwinian theory of the Origin of Species. In the first edition of this book the writer said:

"We are concerned, therefore, not so much with Evolution in its comprehensive sense, as with the specific theory of the origin of living creatures, including man, by a process of 'natural selection' in the 'struggle for existence.'"

It was to the collapse of this part of the whole system, known popularly as "Evolution," that attention was specially directed. A few changes of phraseology have made this distinction clearer in the present edition.

Those who wish to examine further evidence indicative of this movement of philosophic thought away from Darwinism and Materialism, are referred to a work, recently published in Germany, by Professor E. Dennert, Ph.D., entitled *At the Death-bed of Darwinism*, whereof an authorized English translation has been published by the German Literary Board, Burlington, Iowa.

The following quotation from the preface of the translation will indicate the nature and scope of the work:

"In the series of chapters herewith offered for the first time to English readers, Dr. Dennert has brought together testimonies which leave no room for doubt about the decadence of the Darwinian theory in the highest scientific circles in Germany. And outside of Germany *the same sentiment is shared generally by the leaders of scientific thought."*

In chapter ii. of Dr. Dennert's book the testimony of the Strasburg zoologist, Dr Goette, is given, being quoted from his *Present Status of Darwinism*. Dr Goette refers to the reluctance of some naturalists to discard the theory of selection, and says they are disposed to cling to it " simply because it seems to furnish a much desired mechanical explanation of purposive adaptations." This reluctance to discard Darwinism, with nothing but the hated alternative of accepting the Bible account of creation, is quite natural.

Reference may also be had to Professor L. T. Townsend's *Collapse of Evolution* (National Magazine Co., Boston, Mass.), in which the term "Evolution" is used as signifying mainly the Darwinian theory.

But with reference to "Evolution," strictly so-called, the writer not only does not maintain that *that* theory has been generally discarded *in toto,* but, on the contrary, firmly believes that there is a sphere whereof it may truly be said that all things contained therein have, from its very beginning, been subject to, and are still undergoing, never-ceasing changes, and that these changes take place in substantial accordance with the so-called " law of Evolution " as formulated by Herbert Spencer, It was from this sphere that Mr Spencer drew those clear and convincing illustrations of the aforesaid "law" which lent support to his theory, and gained for it such wide acceptance.

The sphere wherein everything, without exception, is uninterruptedly undergoing those evolutionary changes (which Herbert Spencer noted, and which he called " Evolution "), is the sphere of human affairs and activities. Upon surveying this sphere, another observer (not so well known in scientific circles as Herbert Spencer) has summed up the prevailing conditions in the comprehensive and familiar line—

"Change and decay in all around I see."

But the important fact which Mr Spencer and his disciples failed to note is that the operation of the law of Evolution is rigidly limited to the circle of the activities of the descendants of Adam. Within that circle everything, without exception, is subject to evolutionary changes. Outside of it there is nut a trace of such changes. In a word, the area of the operation of the law of Evolution coincides absolutely with the area of the consequences of man's departure from the will of God, as described in Genesis iii. *Evolution is the law of the career of fallen man.* Along the entire pathway of that career, alike in all whereof man boasts and in all whereof he is ashamed, the marks of this law are manifest. Outside of that pathway not a glimpse of it can be seen. This is a fact of tremendous significance, and in order to show its importance the writer has added

Chapters Sixteen to Twenty-Four, inclusive, which did not appear in previous editions.

Philip Mauro.

154, Nassau Street,
New York City.

Chapter One - The Passing of Materialism

THROUGH all generations philosophy has concerned itself with the questions: How did man come to be what he is? and, How did social conditions come to be what they are? These are not really two questions, but one; since the condition of " the world " finds its immediate explanation in human nature.

For thousands of years men have been observing minutely social conditions as they exist from time to time, and the changes from one set of conditions to another. A great mass of facts has been collected and many "laws of nature" have been ascertained or inferred; and upon all this fund of information philosophical minds have pondered, seeking the explanation of man and his world.

The latest and most ambitious attempt at the unification of human knowledge is that made by Mr Herbert Spencer. In the Spencerian view of the universe all changes and developments are, and always have been, controlled by a principle or law of Evolution. According to this supposed law, all developments proceed from the relatively simple and homogeneous to the relatively complex and heterogeneous. Entrusting ourselves to the guidance of this theory we are led backward in time to a condition of extreme simplicity, to a period wherein " eternal and indestructible matter " subsisted in a perfectly simple and undifferentiated condition, and wherein "eternal and indestructible " force had no manifestation, and no property but the impulse to evolve.

This philosophy gives no account of the origin of matter and force, nor does it assume to suggest how the principle of Evolution came into operation. It does not attempt to explain how or by what means the primal impulse to evolve was imparted to matter in its (supposed) primal condition of absolute simplicity and homogeneity. On the contrary, the Spencerian philosophy places the origin of matter, energy, and the primal evolutionary impulse in the region of the "unknowable." It admits the existence of a " First Cause," because the latter is necessary in order to complete the explanation. This " First Cause" is needed for the purpose of starting the universe, and of impressing upon it the primal evolutionary impulse; but thereafter it is dismissed, being *functus officio*, and no longer required for the explanation of phenomena. Lest there should be, on the part of students of this modern philosophy, any disposition to inquire further regarding the " First Cause," that too is placed in the category of the " unknowable."

Spencerian philosophy thus sets itself forth as a finality. Except as to details, it speaks the last words of man's wisdom, since it explains how everything, animate and inanimate, came to be what it is in consequence of gradual changes and of new and ever more complex—but purely spontaneous and fortuitous—groupings of the original atoms; and what it does not purport to explain it puts into the impenetrable region of the " unknowable."

It has been very properly objected that this philosophy is exceedingly unphilosophical in asserting that God (a name which many prefer to " First Cause") *has no power to make Himself known to man*, and that hence the use of the term "unknowable" is wholly unwarranted. The use of this word is simply a presumptuous attempt to erect a barrier against all inquiry into what it most concerns man to know; and from this circumstance alone the truly wise may clearly perceive the origin and purpose of Spencerian philosophy

When once pointed out, it is obvious to the most unphilosophical mind that *God would not be God* if He had not the power to reveal to man so much of Himself, and of His purposes in creation, as the mind of man is capable of comprehending.

We can agree with the conclusions of Herbert Spencer and his school to this extent, that man cannot know anything of his own origin, of human nature with its strange contradictions, and of the existing world-system or organization, *unless it he directly revealed by the Creator.*

Upon this ground "thinkers" of all schools can stand; and their first division must be upon the question whether or not God has communicated with man and given to him a revelation: that is, upon the question—Is the Bible the Word of God?

Chapter Two - The Claim of The Bible

IT has seemed to the writer, after pondering sympathetically the Spencerian explanation of the universe, and after being constrained to recognize its inadequacy, that the Rationalistic method of testing a theory might be applied with helpful results to the Biblical explanation of phenomena. Within recent times the Biblical explanation of the creation of the universe, particularly of the earth and its inhabitants, as given in the first three chapters of Genesis, was rejected by nearly all men who made the slightest pretence to learning, upon the ground that it was in conflict with the supposed facts of natural science.

We do not propose to speak here of the profound change more recently wrought in the attitude of science, in consequence of the latest discoveries of geology and palaeontology. It can now be asserted, upon the authority of the most eminent men of science, that not a single fact stands in contradiction to the Creation story of Genesis. [1] But the question which more nearly concerns us, and which we propose here to consider, is the great question which the philosophy grounded upon Materialism failed utterly to answer, namely: " How did man and the world come to be what they are?" "We are concerned, therefore, not so much with Evolution in its comprehensive sense, as with the specific theory of the origin of the species of living creatures, including man, by a process of " natural selection " in the " struggle for existence."

The time is opportune for such a discussion, because one of the events which is transpiring in our day is the collapse of the Darwinian theory of the Origin of Species. Let us dwell for a moment upon this most impressive fact, and learn from it at least the utter instability of any system of philosophy which has its basis in human wisdom.

Never in the entire history of philosophy was a doctrine more widely accepted among the learned than the Darwinian theory of the Origin of Species. Even doctors of theology and the occupants of Christian pulpits embraced it with real or feigned enthusiasm; and many of these went so far as to declare that it exalted the Creator and inculcated greater reverence for His methods in creation!

So enamoured of this new teaching were these sworn guardians of the " faith once delivered unto the saints " that they readily surrendered all parts of the

Bible which seemed in any way in conflict with it. To accommodate this surrender to their consciences, these compromisers invented the doctrine that "the Bible was not intended to teach science," but was to be accepted and believed only in so far as it related to spiritual and heavenly things; forgetting the words of Christ: "If I have told you *earthly* things and ye believe not, how shall ye believe if I tell you of heavenly things?" (John iii. 12).

That this surrender to the immature and erroneous teachings put forth in the name of science should have had the effect of destroying the faith of many in the whole Scriptures was inevitable. If men be taught that they cannot believe what the Bible says regarding earthly things, how can it be expected that they will believe what it says about heavenly things? Only a few years have passed since the time when, for a man to question the foundations of this doctrine of the Origin of Species was to avow himself a hopeless ignoramus touching the "settled results of science"; and yet to-day the philosophy of Materialism is fast becoming (if it be not so already) a mere historical phase of philosophic thought, to be classified and labelled and put on the shelf, soon to be contemplated merely as a thing which men used to believe.

In the face of this fact it cannot be reasonably supposed that any discoveries which science can make, or any doctrines which philosophy can deduce therefrom, will ever contradict the declarations of Scriptures concerning the creation of the universe by God, the disobedience of the first Adam and the consequent loss of eternal life by all his descendants, and the Divine provision of redemption by new birth into the last Adam. How can we fail to perceive in this history of " Evolution " the truth that a theory which stands merely "in the wisdom of man" has an insecure foundation? Certainly a consideration of the collapse of Darwinism will help us to understand w^hy the inspired Apostle so earnestly desired that the faith of his disciples " should not stand in the wisdom of men, but in the power of God " (1 Cor. ii. 5).

A doctrine which is established in the mind by the force of human arguments can be shaken by like arguments; and it of necessity falls for lack of support when the arguments by which it was bolstered up are forgotten. But the doctrine which rests upon the Word of God has an unfailing support. It needs no argument to sustain it, and none has force enough to overthrow it. The one question upon which reason has to pass judgment is whether the Bible is in fact God's utterance. If it be such, then the things which Spencerian philosophy labels as "unknowable" are not only not unknowable, but are *revealed.* " Eye hath not seen, nor ear heard, neither have entered into the heart of man, the things which God hath prepared for them that love Him, but *God hath revealed them unto us by His Spirit*" (1 Cor. ii. 9, 10).

This Book makes extraordinary claims and extraordinary demands upon men. It does not purport to exhort, advise, or instruct, from the standpoint of superior human wisdom or of superior intelligence or culture. Neither does it seek to commend itself to man's acceptance on the score of expediency, betterment, or progress. In these respects, as in many others, it is radically unlike the writings whereby men seek to help one another. It bases its claim to acceptance *entirely* upon the oft-repeated declaration, " Thus saith Jehovah." It asks no favour of man because of its superior teachings and high standards of life and conduct. The very nature of the Book requires that, if we be logical, we either accept it because " the month of *Jehovah* hath spoken it," or that we cast it aside as the greatest of all *human* impostures.

[1] For a concise and authoritative statement of the attitude of science to-day towards the Creation story, we refer to that valuable booklet, Roger's Reasons, by Rev. John Urquhart, (Marshall Bros.)

Chapter Three - Transformation of Life

BECAUSE the Bible makes such extraordinary demands and statements, it should be most rigorously scrutinized before it be accepted as the Word of God. We may and must assume that the "Word of God will have characteristics whereby it may be distinguished from the word of man; and *a priori* it will be obvious to us that those characteristics will be such that the *unlearned* can distinguish it from all human productions; or, to use the Bible phrase, such that " the wayfaring man, though a fool, shall not err therein."

We shall not here attempt to set forth those characteristics, but will mention only what is perhaps the chief—namely, the power of this Word to transform the life of those who truly accept and believe it.

What lies before the reader in the following pages is an examination of the account which this Book gives us of the conditions of humanity, as they now are and as they have been during all historic times. This account is so radically opposed to the teachings of the philosophy of Materialism, and so repugnant to the natural self-esteem of man, that it would be extremely difficult to account for its presence in any philosophic system which was the product of *human* thought.

We are here confronted by one of the distinguishing characteristics of the Bible. It is the one Book which declares man to be a *fallen* creature, and his world to be a *lost* world. It is the one Book which unsparingly condemns man, which finds "none righteous, no, not one," but all, without any exception, "guilty before God." And yet, instead of being rejected because of these declarations, so offensive to the natural man, the

Bible is the one Book that is translated into every language and dialect, and is read and cherished by some among every nation, tribe, and people. Surely it has required superhuman power to accomplish this!

The Bible itself—its history, its influence, the wonders it has wrought in the lives of men, its power in the world to-day—is an amazing and stupendous fact, for which infidel philosophy has never ventured to offer an explanation, and which it can only ignore. This is but the beginning of the tests which reason, by means of knowledge, may apply to the claims of Scripture. It should, however, suffice, since the only explanation which accounts for the Bible is that it is the "Word of God.

We ask, then, is it possible that the Biblical explanation of man and the world can stand the test of a scrutiny which the Darwinian explanation of the "Descent of Man" could not survive? We confidently assert that the Biblical explanation accounts in a thoroughly satisfactory manner for the present and past conditions of humanity in the mass, and of the nature of the individual human being; and further, we assert that there is now before us, with the facts which recent discoveries have brought into our possession, no explanation which can by any possibility account for the world as it is and has been, excepting that given in Genesis—the Book of Humanity. And if we find this to be indeed the ease, if this ancient explanation survives and prevails to-day over that which so recently dominated the minds of men and was supposed to be based upon all the accumulated knowledge of the ages, must not the reason be that the ancient account came from One who knows all things and needs not that any man should instruct Him?

Chapter Four - The World-System: Its Origin

MAN'S physical organization is such that he cannot obtain, by any investigation he is able to make, the slightest information concerning the causes of social conditions as he finds them in the world, or concerning the origin of the human family, or concerning the end towards which the world movements are hastening. Of these and kindred matters he cannot possibly *know* anything except by Divine revelation.

To speculate touching such matters is foolish and irrational in the extreme; for, apart from revelation, we have no data from which inferences may be drawn, and no possibility of securing such data. Therefore, to one who inquires concerning things spiritual and unseen, concerning the mysteries of sin, sickness, and death, and concerning the tendency of the human heart to evil, the first question to be settled is, Have we a revelation? If he answers that question in the negative, the inquiry is logically at an end.

"We are not here entering upon a discussion of the question whether or not the Bible is true. Even the man who has not for himself decided that question in the affirmative may nevertheless profitably examine the explanation which Holy Scripture gives of the great complex world-system in which he finds himself. After so doing he will be able to test that explanation by the results of bis observation, by the whole state of human affairs as revealed to him in his intercourse with his fellow-men and iu his daily paper, and by what he finds in his own heart. And it may be that, aa the Scriptural explanation sheds its light upon the mysteries and perplexities of human nature and human history, he may not only come to comprehend the mysteries, but may also (which is of greater importance) come to realize that- the light whereby he has explored them is indeed Divine.

Scripture says that the state of humanity in all its phases is the result of an experimental career upon which the parents of the race embarked without the sanction of God and in violation of His express command. It tells us further that the conception of this experiment did not originate with man, but was prompted by a spiritual being of great wisdom and power, who aimed to be man's leader in spiritual matters and to direct his career. We were not told what were the full results which Satan hoped to accomplish by alienating the human race from God and attaching it to himself, but we do know that he seeks to be worshipped (Luke iv. 6, 7; Rev. xiii. 4). It is, moreover, evident that his plan did not disclose as its object the destruction or the injury of the race; but that, on the contrary, he represented himself as solicitous for the well-being of humanity, and for the achievement by it of the best possible results that are attainable *apart from God.*

Because of ignorance of what the Scriptures teach about Satan many people would violently resent the statement that the world is following his leadership. This, however, is not an occasion for a show of resentment. No candid person will deny that the enterprise upon which men are engaged consists essentially in the attempt to organize the best possible world, and to achieve the best possible conditions that can be attained *apart from God.*

Who, then, *is* the god of this world; that is, its spiritual leader and organizer, the person according to whose ideals its activities are planned and its course directed? Satan himself declared that all the kingdoms of the earth and the glory of them are his, and that he can "*give them, to whomsoever he will*" (Luke iv. 5, 6). This is a startling statement, and is not one of his lies, for Scripture repeatedly confirms the statement that Satan is the prince and god of this world (John xii. 31; xiv. 30;

xvi. 11; Acts xxvi. 18; 2 Cor. iv. 4). We wish to grasp the import of this statement, and then to test its probability by our observations of the great and complex world-system which envelops us.

Scripture tells us further that the parents of our race were attracted by the supposed advantages of the career upon which Satan urged them to embark, the chief characteristic of that career (as set forth by the tempter) being the opportunity for *progress or self-improvement through the pursuit and acquisition of knowledge.* The first human pair exercised their power of choice by accepting the career thus offered to them, thereby committing the race to the consequences of that choice, the first consequence being death, or separation from God. Here again we pause to note that the Bible is the only Book which offers an explanation of the stupendous fact of death. Infidel philosophy can but ignore it. "Why should man die? Infidel philosophy can give no answer.

According to Scripture, therefore, we have in the world-system around us the consequence of the acceptance by the human family of Satan's programme and leadership, it having pleased God in His wisdom to permit the working out of this experiment until *His* time shall come for bringing it to its inevitable end.

It is particularly to be observed in the Scripture narrative that the Satanic programme, spread before the first man and woman, contained only what the natural mind adjudges to be a desirable and legitimate object of pursuit. Only one thing stood in the way, namely, a Divine commandment which to all appearance was arbitrary. Under the force of plausible reasoning that restraint was overcome. God's wisdom and His love in imposing it were called in question. Man then, for the first time, set himself to do what he has been prone to do ever since—namely, *to question and pass judgment upon the expediency of a Divine commandment.* He became, in a word, a "higher critic"; that is to say, a man who assumes to criticise the Word of God. Thus it was that the human family entered upon the stupendous experiment of devising a world-system according to Satanic principles.

The account of this momentous event given us in Scripture is exceedingly brief, but every word is charged with a Divine wealth of meaning. The brevity of the account is one of its Divine characteristics, since no human author could have dealt with such an event in that fashion. God does not tell us why, in the moral government of His universe and in the sight of His spiritual creatures, it was necessary that the great human experiment should be suffered to unfold itself through long centuries, until its failure should be demonstrated at every point; but He has seen fit to give us in concise form the history of the event which is the *cause* of all that confronts us in the world around.

Let us study that history, and the more attentively because it is, as a rule, grossly distorted and grievously misunderstood. And let us not fear to scrutinize it with the utmost rigidity, knowing that, if the account be true, we have here *the germ from which all human history*, with its cries and tears, " its oceans of blood and continents of misery," *has unfolded*. If God has given this account, it will not be an allegory. He will not mock us in detailing the tragedy of His creation. If it be true, we shall read its truth in the social conditions of all the ages, and in the nature of each human heart. If it be true, its impress will certainly be observable upon the whole course of human affairs.

Chapter Five - The Seeds of Doubt

THE narrative which we read in the third chapter of Genesis is severe in its brevity and is quite ungarnished. The Narrator described this tremendous event with superhuman simplicity and calmness. He is not man, to delight in the account of great wickedness or of a great calamity. This is the tragedy of the universe, and the heart of God is grieved. Hence, the account is given in the smallest compass. It is devoid of comment, moralizing, or exhortation. There is no attempt to paint the scene, no indication anywhere of the human propensity to heighten the effect by a single superfluous word.

The generation of the doubt. —At the outset God's command is brought under discussion and a question is asked: " Yea, *hath* God said. Ye shall not eat of any tree of the garden?"

Turning from this question to the state of human nature we find that man recognizes himself as a moral creature who is somehow invested with a sense of *accountability.* We find a universal tendency of the heart of man to appease that sense of accountability by debating whether God has really forbidden the desired thing. In the life of every son and daughter of Eve this scene has been many times repeated, with the result that the clearly defined commandment has been lost sight of in the fog of discussion, question, and argument. But this is precisely what we should expect to find if man's present state has resulted from giving entrance to doubt and suspicion of God. Either that is the explanation, or we have none.

The tendency to disbelieve and to question God's Word is undoubtedly the common legacy of the descendants of Adam and Eve. This inherited trait is not usually exhibited in any uncompromising rejection and denial of the Word, but (as in the incident given in the text, whereby the human heart w\as first inoculated with the microbe of unbelief) the inherited trait is usually manifested in the form of a disposition to shade the meaning of the Word, to enlarge or diminish it, or to evade by interpretation, professing all the time a laudable regard for the *spirit* (which may be anything the interpreter likes) as a pretext for disregarding the plain *letter.*

Many religious teachings which find favour with man rely for their acceptance upon *plausibility.* How often we hear the echo of this conversation: "Has God *really* said?" "Surely God, who is all love and tenderness toward His dear children, could never have meant it; for God doth know," etc., etc. This has a very familiar sound. Where did it originate, if not in the scene described in the third chapter of Genesis?

The contradiction. —Doubt having been generated as the result of bringing God's command under discussion, the adversary sets up his own word in direct opposition to what God had said: "Ye shall not surely die, for God doth know that in the day ye eat thereof, then your eyes shall be opened and ye shall be as God, knowing good and evil " (R.V.).

This doctrine is very comprehensive, and its acceptance by the parents of our race has produced effects bearing unmistakably its imprint—effects which are everywhere and most palpably evident in their descendants. The doctrine seeks to gain favour by pretending to defend the character of God against an implication of harshness and severity. " You are unjust to God," says the great questioner, "in supposing that He would visit with death a thing done with a laudable motive." Eternal death is yet disproved to the satisfaction of many by arguments professedly based upon the character of God, upon His love and tenderness. This is a religion that commends itself to the natural heart. It has many forms and millions of adherents today. Small wonder is it that men wish to discard or gloze over that part of the Word of God which says plainly that these religions (though they be termed "Christian") were derived, not from God, but from Satan.

Then again, what trait is there which is more common among men than the inclination to believe the first article in Satan's creed: " Ye shall not surely die"? That article of faith has been incorporated into many of the religious systems of mankind. Its influence may be traced in all the manifold attempts of man to disguise to himself the real nature of death, and in all his attempts to make that grim and hideous enemy—the wages of sin—appear to be something different from what it is.

"There is no death; what seems so is transition," says the poet; and men quote this and like phrases with almost religious fervour. "What is this but an echo of the first lie which was imposed upon mankind? We place flowers on the coffin and speak of the " angel" of death, endeavouring with such vain expedients to disguise the character of this, "the last enemy that shall be destroyed." This lie has, indeed, eaten deeply into human nature, and where is there any explanation of this significant fact, save in the holy Scriptures?

Chapter Six - The Gospel of Self

THE inducement which impelled the woman and the man to commit the forbidden act was the desire for self-improvement. The promise was that they should become God-like.

As we look within and around us we cannot fail to perceive that this inducement is still held out as the great incentive to mankind. The Gospel of Self, and particularly of self-improvement, is vigorously promulgated, not only by the leaders of the world-movements who make no religious professions, but even by " eminent divines." Improve yourself, strive ever upward and onward, make something of yourself, rise to your highest possibilities, get knowledge, *be as gods!* Is not this the burden of the exhortations that are incessantly sounded in the ears of men?

Philosophy takes note of the liability of *repetition* of an act once committed, and of the effect of repetition in the formation of *habit.* What more plausible or satisfactory explanation can we have of this fixed habit of devotion to self-improvement than that given us in the Bible—namely, that it is traced directly back through innumerable repetitions to an act committed at such an early and plastic stage of the race as to influence its entire development?

Put against this the equally striking fact that the Bible is the only Book which directly *opposes* this gospel of self-knowledge and self-improvement, and we have data from which a mind not impaired by the effect of sin could conclusively deduce the Divine authorship of the Bible. Even if uninspired men could conceivably produce a collection of writings containing a central teaching so radically opposed to the deepest-rooted human tendencies, it would yet require an exercise of almighty power to give that Book an influence exceeding that of all other books combined!

Whence, then, came this gospel of self, which is in such direct opposition to the Gospel of Jesus Christ? The existence of the gospel of self-improvement is a fact, and it is the province of philosophy to account for that fact. But again, we have not here a choice between several explanations, any one of which may be the true one. Either that gospel was delivered to the human race in the persons of its parents, or we know nothing about its origin.

And does not the Divine origin of the Gospel of our Lord Jesus Christ appear from its direct opposition to the gospel of the natural man? The teaching of our Lord is to deny self (Matt. xvi. 24; Luke ix. 23), instead of exalting or improving self; not to be as gods, or even "to make a man of oneself," but to " become as little children " (Matt, xviii. 3), He teaches, not *self-reliance*, but self-distrust, and reliance solely upon God. According to His instruction, we are not to develop our faculties to the utmost, but to mortify the members which are on the earth (Col. iii. 5). His witness is ever willing to say "I must decrease" (John iii. 30), even to the very extinction of *self*, until he can joyfully exclaim, *"Not I, but Christ liveth in me"* (Gal. ii. 20).

Just as was done in Eden, this gospel of self-improvement has been proclaimed throughout the ages, and is to-day proclaimed in the name of God Himself, and by those who profess to speak as His Apostles. Of all this we have been duly warned: " For such are *false* apostles, deceitful workers, transforming themselves into the *apostles of Christ.* And no marvel, for Satan himself is transformed into an angel of light. Therefore, it is no great thing if his ministers also be transformed as the ministers of righteousness, whose end shall be according to their works" (2 Cor. xi. 13-15).

The world is peopled to-day by worshippers of the "progress" and "destiny" of humanity—a progress which is effected, and a destiny which is to be achieved, through the very means commended by Satan to our first parents. Even those who try to live according to the Word of God are not free from the disposition to give praise and glory to man for his wonderful achievements, and for the supposed success which has attended his strivings after progress in the direction chosen by the first man at the instigation of Satan.

As we contemplate the complex world-system which has resulted from the zealous pursuit, continued throughout the period of six thousand years, of the Satanic doctrine of self-improvement by the acquisition of knowledge, do we wonder that here and there a voice is raised in appeal for the "simple life'"! And, as has been well said: "What is the simple life but to follow Christ?" The true man of God has always been the man of the tent and the altar. He has no part or interest in the multitudinous affairs, pursuits, interests, and pleasures of the world-system. *His* citizenship is in heaven, and he looks ever ahead to a city that hath foundations, whose Maker and Builder is God, And the only *Perfect* Man who has yet trodden this earth is One who in this world-scheme had not even where to lay His head. He was cut off and had nothing (Dan. ix. 26, E.v.); and on the other hand, He could say, "The *prince of this world* Cometh and hath *nothing in Me"* (.John xiv. 30). The prince of this world had nothing in Him, and He was cut off and had nothing in that world-system whereof Satan is prince. They that are His are content to be like Him in "this present evil world " from which He came to deliver them (Gal. i. 4).

Chapter Seven - As an Angel of Light

(2 Cor. xi. 14)

WITH the acceptance by Adam and Eve of the doctrine presented by Satan and defined in Gen. iii. 5, he became the spiritual and religious leader of the human race. He is still, and through all the ages has been, the religious teacher of every child of Adam who has not been born again of the last Adam. Accustomed as we are to associate the prince of this world chiefly with what is vicious and depraved, and with the crimes and vices to which the baser part of humanity become addicted, we are apt to overlook another aspect of the character of Satan, and to misapprehend the nature of his designs for and upon his subjects. We question if the Devil of Christendom, as generally represented, could ever have gained ascendancy over mankind. But the Devil of Scripture, the highest of all created intelligences, greater even in dignity than the Archangel (Jude 9), *is a very different personage.* The latter is more necessary to the explanation of the condition and history of humanity, and of the contradictions and mysteries of human nature, than is the ether to the explanation of the phenomena of light and electricity.

Not only is belief in the existence of such a spiritual personage a thoroughly rational belief, but, on the other hand, it is irrational to believe otherwise. Xo explanation has ever been brought forward which is capable of accounting for the conditions, contradictions, and mysteries referred to, except that given in the third chapter of Genesis.

The moment we recognize the true character of that being with whom our first parents closed their bargain, we receive light upon the greatest problems that perplex the human soul. The first man, by the exercise of his power of choice, committed the race to Satan's leadership. The latter has done and is doing his very best, not to drag men down, but to *lift men up* and to aid them in working out for them the happiest results. The fact that he has succeeded so well demonstrates his great wisdom and power. The fact that he has not succeeded better demonstrates that his wisdom and power are not those of Deity. That fact proves also that God is *necessary* to the life and welfare of man. This is the first lesson for the individual man.

Satan, doubtless, believed thoroughly in his own system, and in his ability to lead this newly-created race into conditions of self-satisfaction and self-enjoyment. On this assumption we may will believe that he is chagrined and disappointed at the corruption, blemishes, and failures which everywhere appear, and annoyed by the folly and perversity of his followers in choosing vice, crime, and dishonesty in preference to " high ideals " and "noble aspirations." Knowing God in a way that we do not, he could form an estimate of the scope and chances he would have in assuming the leadership of this race, should he succeed in attaching it to himself. What he could not foresee was, first, the follies into which the poor, helpless creatures would blunder when deprived of communion with God; and second, the marvellous work of redemption which Infinite wisdom would evolve and Infinite love would execute.

Consider the results of this great experiment, this joint-adventure of Devil and man, as those results are spread before our eyes! Surely they are great and impressive in their abundance and variety; and notwithstanding all the failures, disappointments and ruins, and all the sad, dark, and ugly features which cannot be hidden out of sight, we must admit that "the god of this world" is a personage of great intelligence and resourcefulness.

The world-system, apart from God's agencies and people, *who are in hut not of it,* is marvellous in its complexity and detail, as well as in the character and variety of its activities. Its grandeur is undeniable, and it challenges our admiration; although we perceive everywhere an incurable tendency in the various parts of the system to fall into disarrangement, disorder, and decay.

This wonderful system has worlds within worlds. We hear of the world of business, the world of politics, the world of fashion, the world of pleasure, the world of science, the world of sport, the world of finance, the world of music, the world of literature; the dramatic world, the social world, the industrial world, the commercial world, the religious world. Everyone can have a share! This prodigious world-system includes monarchies, republics, despotisms, laws, customs, traditions, corporations, syndicates, trusts, banks, clubs, brotherhoods, colleges, theatres, race tracks, gambling-halls, trades unions, philanthropies, liquor saloons, brothels, inebriate homes and cures, sanitariums, reformatories, temperance societies, gaols, libraries, cemeteries, insane asylums, courts, legislatures, lobbies, stock markets, department stores, insurance companies, newspapers, magazines, automobiles, philosophies, fashions, cults, factories, railroads, navies, armies, high explosives, diplomacies, peace tribunals, hypnotism, spiritualism, Christian Science, Higher Criticism, New Thought, and religious systems to suit every shade of opinion. To all these and other restless, stirring, feverish activities, organizations and contrivances, is given the imposing title of **"Civilization,"** whose glorious mission is to go forward and conquer the earth for man. [1]

In such a system it should be possible to suit everyone. There is something for the moral man, something for the religious man, something for the thoughtful man, something for the benevolent man, something for the ambitious man, something for the industrious man, something for the cultured man, something for the idle man, something for the vicious man. In a word there is something for everyone, *with a single exception*. In the entire system there is nothing for God's Perfect Man. For Him this system had nothing; no place at the inn, no place to lay His head—nothing but a manger, a cross, and a tomb. Between Him and this world-system there was *nothing in common*. Consequently, when the time arrived for Him to say, "This is your hour and the power of darkness" (Luke xxii. 53), the leaders and representatives of the world's culture, the world's intelligence, the world's progress, the world's power, and the world's religion, led Him with expressive ceremony " outside the camp" and nailed Him to the tree. *"And sitting down they watched Him there"* (Matt, xxvii. 36).

And now, patient reader, who have read thus far—perhaps merely from curiosity to see how the writer sustains a somewhat novel proposition—let me put a question in deep seriousness: What do you think of "this world," you who perhaps call yourself by the name of that crucified One? Are you quite sure that you are not one of that religious throng who, on that day (and ever since) have considered Him only to the extent of turning aside during a brief period of leisure in order to contemplate, while sitting at ease, the spectacle of His dying agonies'? To what extent are your hopes and interests wrapped up in this evil world,, whose leaders placed Him there; and how far are your affections set upon it? How much of *yourself* would perish if this world-system were swept off the earth the next moment? Is there any possibility that you, too, are an indifferent spectator of the scene which the world enacted on Calvary?—that scene wherein were revealed both the true nature of the world and also the limit of the love of God?

And you, all you others who do not call yourselves "Christians," yet who cannot avoid seeing, however much you may try, that Figure nailed to the cross, " is it nothing to you, all ye that pass by?" Indeed, it is *everything* to you.

That, indeed, was *their hour* and the power of darkness. His hour had not yet come; *but it is coming.* As surely as we have had Satan's leadership and the very best world that men could fashion upon his principles, so surely will we have Jesus Christ and a world arranged and governed upon His principles. " Be patient, therefore, brethren, unto the coming of the Lord" (James v. 7).

[1] In this connection, however, see Divine Agencies in the World (chap. xiv.).

Chapter Eight - The Failure of The Scheme

TRULY, this world-system is a marvellous affair—stupendous, gigantic, remorseless, terrifying! Seemingly composed entirely of human elements, it is yet strangely unmanageable and perverse in human hands. If we study any number of the individual human beings of which this prodigy is composed, we shall be utterly unable to discover in them an explanation of some of its characteristics and of its behaviour as an organization.

Though composed apparently *of* human beings and existing presumably *for* human beings, it nevertheless devours men, women, and children placidly and for trifling considerations. Society will do what individual members of society would be incapable of doing. The world has been aptly compared to a slave-ship in which a few favoured passengers dance and make merry on deck, utterly oblivious of the groans of a dense mass of suffering humanity beneath.

Those who occupy the positions of worldly advantage are for ever soliciting the admiration of mankind at large for this gigantic world-machine. They never tire of calling attention to the wonders of its construction and operation, and to the many ingenious improvements which are from time to time introduced into it. To bow down and worship the Thing is, with many, an act of religion; and the multitude are intellectually sand-bagged into accepting the doctrine of the " progress of man."

If anyone ventures to question this creed, and to call attention to facts tending to show that the progress of the world is not upward, but downward, he is instantly denounced as a " pessimist" to whom no heed should be paid.

And yet observers do note that the machinery of the vast affair creaks fearfully at times, and manifests strain at every joint; that there is a woeful lack of harmony and co-ordination among the various parts, and that only by the most vigilant attention and by incessant repairs is the thing kept in operation at all! It is undeniable that, in spite of expedients and experiments, and of all the care and labour bestowed upon the affair, its parts are constantly getting out of gear, and working havoc with human life and human projects.

The only reason why the centrifugal forces of evil have not long ago disrupted the whole affair is because their tendencies have been checked by the Divine agencies which are in the world, but not of it. These restraining influences are reserved for consideration in a later chapter; but it is pertinent here to remind the reader that he " who now hindereth will hinder until he be taken out of the way," and that then shall come the full disclosure of evil in the person of "that wicked one " (2 Thess. ii. 7, 8).

Why, then, notwithstanding the manifest imperfections and failures of the system, does the gospel of " progress" find such ready acceptance among men? Upon the assumption of the truth of Scripture the answer is clear and satisfactory. It is because that is the gospel which was accepted by humanity at the beginning of its present career. Having chosen it, man is reluctant to confess that he committed a fatal blunder in so doing. He rather clings to it with all the tenacity of superstition, and tries to persuade himself that he likes the result of his choice.

But even so, the true character and tendency of the world-system would be recognized by the majority of thoughtful men and women, if they were not under the blinding influence of the egregiously erroneous notion that *God, and not Satan, is running the world.* Ignorant but well-meaning persons evolve such pleasing sentiments as that " God's in His heaven, all's well with the world"; or they misquote (by partly quoting) Romans viii. 28, saying that "all things work together for good"; and the careless multitudes accept these as Bible truths. There is no deliverance from the bondage of such errors except in embracing the truth clearly taught in Scripture— that Satan, and not Jehovah, is the god of this present evil age; and that Satan, not Jehovah, is directing its present activities. This teaching accounts completely for everything which, on any other hypothesis, is mysterious and perplexing.

The god of this gigantic world-system displays great ingenuity and fertility in devising new expedients for temporarily curing the innumerable defects which crop out in all parts of the organization. We see activity on all sides, a patient building up of one place while another falls into decay, a never-ceasing but never-successful effort to prevent the decay of nations, the failures of government, the oppressive use of power, the moral decay of the prosperous classes, and the universal spread of selfishness and corruption. Chiefly are the activity and ingenuity of Satan exercised in the multitude of expedients whereby the minds of men are occupied and diverted from contemplating and inquiring into the reason of the inherent rottenness of the world-system and the certainty of its ultimate destruction.

It is evident enough to those who will but give themselves a chance to think, that *something is vitally wrong with the system*. Death is intrenched at its heart. Crime and cruelty and misery in many forms pervade it. Nothing is permanent. " Change and decay in *all* around we see." The presence of these grim advance-agents of destruction is detected in all things wherein man has a part. Yet somehow the presiding genius of this world-system contrives to keep men busy in one way and another, and to keep alive the delusion that, as a general proposition, " things are getting better."

Thus do the sons of Adam continue to exhibit their inherited predisposition to the acceptance of that pleasing doctrine: "Ye shall not surely die; ye shall be as God."

How admirably are all these world-activities and occupations (which those who should know better are accustomed to ascribe to Almighty God) calculated to accomplish the great Satanic purpose of hiding from men the Gospel of Jesus Christ! How admirably do they serve the end of confirming men in the fatal belief that humanity does not need a Saviour! Let anyone try to conceive a state of things which would better accomplish this object than that state of things which prevails in the world to-day, and he will speedily give it up as an impossibility.

How illuminating then are the words of the Apostle in 2 Cor. iv. 3, 4:—"But if our gospel be hid, it is hid to them that are lost" (or rather, as in the R.V., "them that are perishing"), in whom the *god of this world* hath blinded the minds of them which believe not, lest the light of the glorious gospel of Christ, who is the image of God, should shine unto them."

This is the meaning of it all; and we never could have discovered that meaning for ourselves. God alone could reveal it to us. But now that He has done so, we are without excuse if we refuse to believe Him; and we have miserably failed in the use of our natural intelligence if it does not, upon examination of the conditions around us, confirm His revelation.

Chapter Nine - The Bible Solution

IT is entirely safe to assert that, if any infidel or agnostic philosophy offered an interpretation of the world which explained the facts so clearly as does this Scriptural explanation, it would have received and would have retained universal acceptation. Why, then, is the explanation given in the Bible so widely rejected? Here, again, we have an extraordinary phenomenon, and we must look into God's Word to ascertain that this is another effect of the fall of man—namely, the inherited tendency of the natural heart to unbelief. Yes, the vast system spread over the earth is a, *perishing* system, containing in itself the seeds of decay. " The world passeth away, and the lust thereof" (1 John ii. 17). That fact is plain enough without the statement of Scripture. But what if it be also true, as the Scripture declares, that they who commit themselves to this system and its leader shall surely perish with it and with him!

Are you, my reader, trusting for your safety to your good character, to your pure motives and kindly deeds; or are you perhaps trusting to the chance that it will all "come right somehow"? Is your heart occupied with the affairs of this world, its projects and ambitions, and are you for your future happiness looking forward to the working out of some detail of the world-system? This (unless Scripture lies in its central part) is the *very purpose* of that world-system; whereas the purpose of God is that our hearts should be occupied with the invisible and eternal things, and our outlook should be for the glorious appearing of the great God and our Saviour Jesus Christ (Titus ii. 13).

In Scripture, then, we find a complete answer to every question which arises in the mind concerning the presence, at all times and everywhere in human nature and human affairs, of sin, sickness, and death, and concerning the presence in the world of accidents, corruption, and decay. The answer to every such question is that this is not God's world, but Satan's. The characteristics which we observe in the world's organization, and in the way in which its functions are discharged, are just such as would be expected in an organization planned and managed by a personage such as the Satan of Scripture is described to be— namely, a fallen spiritual being of consummate wisdom, the highest of all created intelligences, the head of vast powers and principalities, but coming short of the power and wisdom of Deity, and existing in a state of rebellion against God.

The great truth that Satan is "the god of this world," which is absolutely needed for the understanding of the existence of evil in the world, and which Almighty God has revealed for the very purpose of guarding us from the manifold dangers arising out of ignorance of it, is missed by many who accept the Bible as the Word of God. These are consequently in much danger and in needless perplexity because of the abundant manifestations of evil and imperfection in the world. In the light of this important truth, all such perplexity disappears, since it is obvious that those grievous things, for whose presence we could not account in God's world, are quite in place in Satan's world.

We read in Scripture that the *earth* is the Lord's and the fulness thereof. He sends the rain and the sunshine, and gives the increase of the field and the fruits of the earth. But the *world* is Satan's. His ownership of the world, so far from being questioned by Scripture, is strongly asserted and acknowledged. Satan displayed to our Lord *"all the kingdoms of the world* and the glory of them" (Matt. iv. 8), and offered to give them to Him upon one condition. The Lord refused the offer, but did not question the ownership. Consequently the world is still Satan's. The Lord Jesus acknowledged this at a later time, saying, " The Prince of this world cometh and hath nothing in Me " (John xiv. 30), and the last of His apostles, near the close of his long life, described the condition of affairs, saying, " The *whole world* lieth in the evil one" (1 John v. 19, r.v.). The Lord Jesus declared that the world hated Him because He "testified of it that its *works are evil*" (John vii. 7). He did not distinguish or bestow praise on any of the works of this world-system upon which men pride themselves, but pronounced them all uncompromisingly and unequivocally *evil.* The man who dares do that is still hated.

It is well at this point to have in mind a further and very striking characteristic of this great organization which we call "the world." That men should admire it is natural, considering the part which men have played in elaborating and running it; but each individual knows full well that the part he has performed has been largely forced. He has been only to a very limited extent a free agent, feeling always, and frequently recognizing, *the force of some one, or some thing, unseen and yet potent in the affairs of the world.*

This is clearly recognized in that very common expression " the force of circumstances." What *is* the force referred to in this conventional phrase 1 Our object is to identify the person or the thing by whom or by which is exerted the force that makes the world what it is, and that compels men and women to act as they do. Therefore, we take due note of the many evidences of great wisdom, ingenuity, skill and energy which are displayed in the conduct of the world's affairs. We must acknowledge that, by these indications, the great ability of the presiding genius of the world's affairs is fully established.

But our observations do not stop there. The evidences on every side of want of foresight, and of failure to anticipate undesirable events and to provide for emergencies, are too numerous and too striking to be overlooked. They are also much too serious to be made light of. Nations arm themselves and make war against other nations; men oppress their fellows; society separates into hostile clashes, whereof the upper stratum can always hear the mutterings of the discontented and oppressed beneath; trusted officials of financial institutions default or enrich themselves by fraudulent practices; commercial organizations thrive by systematic knavery; legislation is almost openly bought and sold; municipal corruption increases; and social morals decay with the increase of wealth and culture.

Looking backward through the eyes of history to the events of past generations, we observe that —while man has always tried to put the best face upon the social condition of his day, and has always given the most favourable account of his times—nevertheless, *failure* has been ever the record of the human race. Nations rise and fall; and whenever another fair experiment in government is attempted, under new conditions and with all past experience for a guide, it is only a matter of time before the very ends sought for— increase of wealth and power—show that they are but agents of destruction.

What can explain all this so clearly as the fact that the god and prince of this world, with all his transcendent abilities, lacks the power and wisdom of the Infinite?

As we write these lines, the attention of the public is being drawn to surprising revelations of dishonesty in the management of large insurance companies, revelations which would certainly shock the moral sense of the community if the community had any residuum of moral sense to be shocked. One who looks at all beneath the surface of these shameful disclosures cannot fail to realize that they are but indications, surface eruptions, of *diseased conditions* which lie deep in human nature and human society. Once again, as in the days before the Flood, the Lord God, looking down from heaven, sees that " all flesh has corrupted its way upon the earth." Is it not so?

And is it not also true that the very worst and most significant feature of these revelations is that they produce little or no expression of deep or widespread public indignation? A few caustic editorials appear in the newspapers, and a few denunciations are heard from the pulpit; but the people, as a whole, are indifferent, unmoved, or what is even worse, are merely entertained.

Meanwhile, the blind and fatuous leaders of the enterprises of the age and the exponents of the much-lauded "spirit of the age" continue to prate of progress and improvement, of the conquests of civilization and of the great strides of science! Only the few who have sought and obtained wisdom from the sole Source of wisdom recognize that the state of things around us now is "as it was in the days of Noah."

And this is the outcome of the free application of human genius and intelligence, backed up by the amplest natural resources and aided by every factor which is supposed to make for progress!

What conclusion is to be drawn from it, and what remedy is to be applied? We hear " enticing words of men's wisdom," such as " legislation," "education," "culture," "publicity," "honest enforcement of laws," etc. But who is so shallow and ignorant as not to know that these have all been tried, have done their utmost, *and have failed*? The corruption now appearing in the "highest circles," where education and culture have done their utmost, where every experiment of legislation has been attempted, and where every natural incentive to honest dealing exists, has its source *in the heart of man*. It flows from that fountain of sin which sprang from the transgression of the first Adam, and which can be purified only by the fountain of life which springs from the blood of the last Adam.

What sane conclusion, then, is possible but this, that man's experiment has been tried out *to the very end*? And what remedy remains, but that which the arrogant and unbelieving heart has always sought to avoid, but which God has always urged in such words as these: " Look unto Me and be ye saved, all the ends of the earth; for I am God, and there is none else" (Isa, xlv. 22) 1 And do we not see written large and clear upon the events of our day that but little time remains wherein to learn wisdom, to heed the oft-repeated warnings, and to turn unto Him before He leaves His mediatorial throne, before the day of grace is ended, and He comes again to shake terribly the earth?

At this moment the chief executive of the American nation, in the course of a series of speeches, feels called upon to take notice of these things, and here is his comment upon them:

"The man of great means who achieves fortune by crooked methods does wrong to the whole body politic. But he not merely does wrong to, he becomes a source of imminent danger to, other men of great means, for his ill-won success tends to arouse a feeling of resentment, which, if it becomes inflamed, fails to differentiate between the men of wealth who have done decently and the men of wealth who have not done decently.

"The conscience of our people has been deeply shocked by the revelations made of recent years as to the way in which some of the great fortunes have been obtained and used; and there is, I think, in the minds of the people at large a strong feeling that a serious effort must be made to put a stop to the cynical dishonesty and contempt for right which have thus been revealed. I believe that something, and I hope that a good deal, can be done by law to remedy the state of things complained of.

"But when all that can be has thus been done, there will yet remain much which the law cannot touch, and which must be reached by the *force of public opinion*." (Speech of President Roosevelt, Oct. 2, 1905.)

The fact, however, is that the conscience of our people has *not* been shocked in the slightest by these revelations, and the best that a well-meaning man, imbued with the so-called optimism of the time, can give us is the hollowest of conventional phrases, the futile suggestion (in which he can hardly believe himself) that something "can be done by law to remedy the state of things complained of," and the reluctant confession that there will yet remain " much which the law cannot touch." It is safe to say that not one intelligent person who reads this comment upon the *most important existing condition of our national life* will have the least confidence in the remedial effect of "the force of public opinion," to which dubious agency our President commits this hideous and loathsome disease in the vitals of the body politic. It would be just as sensible to rely upon the force of public opinion to arrest and turn back the ravages of cholera or smallpox. But what else can be suggested? Would it not seem that men would be compelled at last to appeal to the power of God, if only because of the manifest failure of every other remedy? Will anyone say that it is the act of a rational and enlightened mind to look rather to the force of public opinion than to the return of our Lord from heaven to bring in everlasting righteousness? Are we not at last justified in receiving this as our "blessed hope," and acknowledging that there is none beside?

Chapter Ten - "Fig Leaves"

THE promise of Satan began immediately to be fulfilled, though not, we may be sure, in the manner understood and expected by his dupes. The woman ate of the fruit, and the man, who apparently stood by during the colloquy (for the account says that she gave unto her husband, who was with her), immediately followed her example. The man apparently was prudent and willing to listen to, without taking part in, the discussion between the woman and the first higher critic of the Word of God. Apparently he watched her experiment, and, seeing that no visible harm followed, imitated her action. Have we here the explanation of woman's influence over man in spiritual matters and in affairs wherein the affections are concerned? The result was, indeed, the immediate acquisition of knowledge. " The eyes of them both were opened, and they *knew that they were naked*."

Moreover, this newly-acquired knowledge was immediately applied to practical use, and mankind forthwith entered upon its career of activity. "And they sewed fig-leaves together and made themselves aprons."

In this short sentence the Divine source of the narrative may be clearly perceived by all who have eyes to see. The two concise statements of this sentence set forth the subjective and objective consequences flowing from man's disloyalty to God and his acceptance of the leadership of Satan. Contained within this brief sentence, which is devoid of comment and phrased with superhuman simplicity, is an epitome of human nature and human history. What the man and woman immediately acquired was the now predominant trait of *self-consciousness.* "They saw that they were naked." Previously they were naked, but " were *not* ashamed" (Gen. ii. 25).

God-consciousness has now been lost, and in its place has come *self*-consciousness; and henceforth self-contemplation is to be the characteristic and bane of mankind, laying tlie foundation for those inner feelings or mental conditions comprehended under the term " unhappiness," and for all the external strivings whereby effort is made to attain a better condition.

And what are all these efforts and activities but further endeavours of the same sort as the very first human effort, which history has thus recorded for us, after man's departure on his career of self-reliance? Is it not plain that the act here recorded is the germ of all subsequent human activities? Becoming conscious of self, and of his deficiencies, no longer having a present God to supply all necessities, and being, moreover, under the delusion of the possibility of better conditions, man begins to invent and contrive. He makes himself an apron to cover his nakedness; and this has been the occupation of his descendants to the present day. The occupation thus handed on from generation to generation takes a great variety of forms, but through them all the nature and object of the occupation remain the same.

Man was obviously not made for self-contemplation, but rather to look away from himself. This is apparent from his very anatomy. Man is, as to all his vital organs, practically hidden from himself. The important functions of the body are carried on by concealed apparatus and engines, marvellous contrivances whose operations and processes still, after all these centuries of self-examination, remain unsolvable mysteries. The processes of the mind are absolutely inscrutable to the mind itself. The senses are adapted to giving man information concerning external things; but concerning themselves, or how they transmit information from without, they can tell him practically nothing. Consciousness, that mysterious reservoir wherein is gathered all man's knowledge, contains no knowledge whatever of its own nature. What a calamity, therefore, has befallen a creature so organized, in becoming *self*-centred and addicted to *self*-contemplation!

To this cause we may trace all morbid, unwholesome, and depressing mental states. This is commonly recognized, and yet despite his own efforts and despite all the manifold contrivances wherewith the world is equipped, how difficult it is for the natural man to avoid lapsing into self-contemplation! Indeed, knowing nothing better, nothing higher and more important than *self,* his thoughts must naturally gravitate to that object as a centre when released from the control of the will. There is nothing more attractive than childhood in its freshness and *unconsciousness of self;* but when self-consciousness begins, the charm disappears. Do we not see in this the profound reason why the Lord Jesus Christ pointed to a " little child" as the type of those who shall compose His Kingdom?

And what is it that spurs men along the many lines of human activity? Is it not the same subjective condition which prompted the making of the apron of fig-leaves—namely, man's consciousness of some deficiency, and the desire to supply it by his own efforts'? This is only putting in another form the oft-stated incentive to human exertion—namely, the so-called " duty" of the individual to develop what is in him, and thus to rise to his " highest possibilities."

There is, indeed (and it must not be ignored, because it comes from God Himself), another reason for activity on man's part—namely, the daily recurring needs of the body. God declared it as one of the consequences of man's disobedience that in the sweat of his face he should eat bread. But this is not the career, nor was it included in the career, Divinely appointed for man. On the contrary, it is a penal consequence of his departure from the Divinely appointed career. Man does not by any natural impulse accept, nor does he without protest accept, the " gospel of work." It is not God's "Word that declares incessant toil to be the purpose for which he was created. This, again, is a doctrine which proceeded from a very different source.

Moreover, it is one thing to labour for the necessities of the mortal body, and it is another and very different matter to labour for the success of Satan's world-scheme. Following but a short way down the stream of human history which had its source in the Garden of Eden, we observe that it was Cain's descendants who builded a city, who invented metal-working, who devised musical instruments, and who first composed poetry in praise of the doings of man (Gen. iv. 17-24)

Those whose occupation is " to serve the living and true God and to wait for His Son from heaven " (1 Thess. i. 9, 10) have no share in the occupation which absorbs the great mass of humanity—namely, the futile attempt to make earth a satisfactory habitation for man *apart from God*. Recognizing that the experiment to which Adam committed his family was the attempt to achieve a destiny without Divine aid, those who have received the truth of God into their hearts, and have been made thereby wise unto salvation, understand that the end will be a failure which will be recognized by all in the light of His presence, and the destruction of all the works that men have so laboriously wrought.

Chapter Eleven - "Where Art Thou?"

IF, then, one admits the truth of God into his heart, which every man may do if he will, the real state of the world's affairs will be made plain to him; and he will understand from the drift of those affairs, as well as from the revelation of God in the Scriptures, the end to which the world is hastening. His concern will then be to know if God has a remedy.

Manifestly, our knowledge of God's remedy can come only through revelation; and again we are confronted by the fact that, if the Bible be not God's written word, we have no revelation, and consequently no remedy. The inquiry, therefore, cannot be pursued except upon the assumption that the Bible is God's revelation to His creature, man. If that Word be true, then we know that God began immediately after man's departure to sock his recovery; and the unfolding of the Divine plan of redemption is most satisfying to the regenerated mind and heart.

The very first words of Him whose holy law had been broken and whose love had been suspected and spurned, reveal Him as seeking His fallen creature. "Where art thou?" is the question; and from that moment to the present we have the redemption of man proclaimed as the purpose of Jehovah, to be fulfilled in the person of the Eternal Son, who in the fulness of time came " to seek and to save that which was lost" (Luke xix. 10). He came also to destroy the works of the Devil (1 John iii. 8); and since man learned his way from the Devil, we are not surprised to learn that God's ways are very different: " For My thoughts are not your thoughts, neither are your ways My ways, saith Jehovah " (Isa. Iv. 8).

Accordingly, He bids us no longer to contemplate self, but to contemplate *Him* —"looking unto Jesus" (Heb. xii. 2), to "consider the Apostle and High Priest of our profession, Christ Jesus " (Heb. iii. 1), and to look "not at the things that are seen, but at the things that are not seen " (2 Cor. iv. 18). He bids us to cease from the vain attempt at the improvement of the old nature, which cannot be made fit for the presence of God, but is hopelessly corrupted and doomed to death, and offers instead to all who believe on Him a new nature, "born not of corruptible seed, but of incorruptible " (1 Pet i. 23); for " if any man be in Christ, he is a *new creature*" (2 Cor. v. 17). He bids us cease from the futile attempt at supplying our own deficiencies and covering ourselves with our own righteousness; for Christ is of God made unto us righteousness (1 Cor. i. 30). He would have us all, as did His servant Paul, count all things that the world can offer us as refuse, in order that we may gain Christ and be found in Him, not having a righteousness of our own, but that which is from God by faith, that we may *know Him*, and the power of His resurrection, and the fellowship of His sufferings, becoming conformed unto His death (Phil. iii. 8-10).

In one word, God's remedy for the havoc wrought by the first Adam is *Christ,* the last Adam, in whom all the purposes of God in the creation of man will be fulfilled, and in whom all the promises of God are Yea and Amen (2 Cor. i. 20).

God assures us that He Himself has undertaken and accomplished the *work* of redemption, and that our part is, not to work, but to *believe* and accept the work done for us. For justification is, "to him that worketh not, but believeth on Him that justifieth the ungodly" (Rom. iv. 5); or, as elsewhere stated by our Lord Himself: " This is the work of God, that ye *believe* on Him whom He hath sent" (John vi. 29). The original sin was unbelief and distrust. Eve disbelieved in her *heart.* Hence belief truth the heart is the turning point of man's conversion (Rom. x. 10). Man must turn with his heart to God and confess the crucified and risen Saviour. More than this is not required for salvation, *but less will not serve.*

It is possible, alas! to have an intellectual comprehension of all this, and yet not be united with Christ by the Spirit of God. One may arrive at the conclusion, upon examination of the conditions within and around him, that the record of Genesis is, indeed, that of an actual historical event. lie may even thereby become satisfied that the Scriptures are inspired throughout; and yet he may have no real knowledge of Christ, and may belong wholly to this perishing world. For saving faith is of the heart. One must be brought by the Spirit of God under conviction of sin (the sin of unbelief), and be born again by acceptance of Jesus Christ as the Saviour, and as the one and only way of coming to the Father.

The foregoing pages have not been written for the purpose merely of vindicating the historical character of the third chapter of Genesis. To convince the intellect of the reader as to this would be of no advantage, unless the conviction goes further and reaches his *heart.* The best and most convincing of human arguments affords no certainty to the mind and no peace to the soul. One may to-day be persuaded by argument to give intellectual assent to a doctrine, and begin to doubt its truth to-morrow when the steps of the argument that wrought conviction slip from his memory. The Word of the Living God alone can impart absolute conviction and afford a permanent basis for certainty. When belief in the Lord Jesus Christ, the incarnate Word of God, is wrought in the heart by the operation of the Holy Spirit, faith comes to abide eternally; for it is accompanied by such a work of grace, such conviction and light, and such manifestations of Divine Presence and power, that the heart necessarily surrenders itself with full confidence to His keeping.

"I give unto them eternal life, and they shall never perish, and no one shall snatch them out of My hand " (John x. 28).

Nevertheless, an appeal to the reason should not be in vain; for, as the result of intellectual conviction, one may be induced to act upon the truth which has been intellectually apprehended. The object of these pages, therefore, is to rouse the indifferent and callous soul to action—to the making of a choice between Satan's world and God's, between the way of life and the way of death. "Behold," says Jehovah, "I set before you the way of life and the way of death " (Jer. xxi. 8). You have a will, my friend, and you have the power to exercise it in this matter. If persuaded in your mind of the truth of God's Word, or if only partly persuaded, call upon Him! Say, "Lord, I believe: help Thou mine unbelief! " Ask Him to show you whether these things be true, to give you His Holy Spirit according to the promise (Luke xi. 13), and to reveal the Lord Jesus to you, not only as the Saviour of the world, but also as the Saviour of your individual soul. Ask Him for *faith*, which is not, as many seem to suppose, believing something without foundation, but is the very "*evidence* of things not seen" (Heb. xi. 1), evidence of the highest value because proceeding from God Himself.

"Where, then, is *the seat of faith*? Not in the intellect, which sees the logical connexion or the historic evidence; nor in the imagination, which recognizes the beauty and organic symmetry, and reproduces the pictures; not in the conscience, which testifies to the righteousness and truth of the revelation: but in a something which lies deeper than these, in which all these centre, and to which all these return. It is with the heart, as Scripture teaches, that man believeth. There, whence are the issues of life—emotional, intellectual, moral, spiritual—in that secret place to which God alone has access, God's Word as a seed begets *faith,* God's Word as a light kindles light, and the *man* becomes a *believer*" (Saphir).

Such is the nature of saving faith, which all may have who will seek it from the Author of faith, and which they only who possess it can comprehend. We cannot impart our faith to another, but we can witness to God who gave it, and can tell to others how they may obtain "a like precious faith with us in the righteousness of our God and Saviour, Jesus Christ" (2 Pet. i. 1).

Chapter Twelve - The Deceiver of The World

SATAN is given, among other descriptive titles, that of " the *deceiver* of the whole world" (Rev. xii. 9, R.V.). Jesus Christ is truth, life, and light. Satan is deception, darkness, and death. The world, as now organized, is full of " the deceivableness of unrighteousness." In order to have the capability of deception, the spurious thing must closely imitate the genuine. A lie does not deceive unless it has the guise of truth. The deceptive contrivance or device, in order to fulfil the object of its author, must have the promise and appearance of desirable properties while lacking the substance thereof.

The characteristic of deceitfulness may be discovered in Satan's world-scheme at whatever point it may be closely scrutinized. Scripture speaks of the "deceitfulness of riches" (Matt. xiii. 22), and this may well serve as the typical illustration of the subject, because there is in our day no other object so prominently set up by men before their own eyes as worthy of their most strenuous efforts, no other object in the ardent pursuit of which so many human beings are intently engaged as the acquisition of money. From generation to generation man's experience has uniformly witnessed to the truth of the Scriptural statement touching the deceitfulness of riches; and yet the power of deception therein was never greater in its intensity or more disastrous in its results than at the present day. The amassing of colossal fortunes is one of the striking characteristics of the age. Men are, indeed, heaping up their treasure in the last days (James v. 3). No natural explanation will account for the deceptive power of riches. It can only be understood in the light of the explanation of Scripture that Satan is the god—that is to say, the architect, constructor, and engineer—of this world-system, and that his character inheres in his work.

But let the scrutinizing gaze of the inquirer be directed to any other object which the director of the world's affairs places before the minds of men, and he will perceive that the same quality of deceitfulness resides in them all. The apostle speaks of the "deceitfulness of sin " (Heb. iii. 13) and of its *hardening* effect upon the nature of man. This brief word of Scripture is a veritable searchlight whereby the depths of human nature and the very core of the world-system may be explored.

It is beyond question a ray of the "true light." Sin is deceitful, and men are beyond controversy hardened thereby. The truth of this appears on all sides.

Is there, then, no one to whom we may go; no one in whom there is no deceit and no darkness at all? Yes, there is One, even He of whom God says, " This is My beloved Son, hear Him." And if we heed this command and listen to His words, what do we hear Him say concerning this world through which we are now passing] He has many things to say on this subject, solemn, pointed, urgent words. He says that it shall not profit a man if he gain the whole world and lose his own soul (Matt. xvi. 26). He says that if we are of the world the world will love us, for it loves its own; but that they who are His are not of the world, because He has chosen them out of the world, and that therefore the world hates them (John XV, 19). He says that if the world hates us we may know that it *hated Him* before it hated us (v. 18). He foretold that the world would rejoice at His death (John xvi. 20), and declared that His disciples were not of the world, even as He was not of the world (John xvii. 14). The Apostle who was closest to His heart gives us a picture of the men of the world and the theme of their talk, saying, " They are of the world, therefore *speak they of the world, and the world heareth them*" (1 Juhn iv. 5). "Whoever has something to say in praise of the world, however false his flatteries may be, is sure of an audience. And through the same Apostle God speaks these piercing words:—

"Love not the world, neither the things that are in the world. If any man love the world, the love of the Father is not in him. For all that is in the world, the lust of the flesh, and the lust of the eyes, and the vainglory of life, is *not* of the Father, but is *of the world.* And the world passeth away, and the lust thereof; but he that doeth the will of God abideth for ever" (1 John ii. 15-17, R.V.).

What can this be but the direct consequence of the event described in the third chapter of Genesis? All the outward manifestations of evil in the world are classed under three heads. These manifestations have no explanation, and are absolutely incomprehensible without the event recorded in that chapter. With it "all that is in the world" is intelligible. The mother of all mankind " saw that the tree was good for food "—the lust of the flesh; "and that it was a delight to the eyes" — the lust of the eyes; "and that the tree was to be desired to make one wise "—the vainglory of life.

Is it possible for any rational man, after paying the slightest attention to these scriptures, and perceiving but a small fraction of the magnitude and universality of the truth contained in these few words, to doubt that they are from God? Surely it must be plain, upon the briefest consideration, that no man could have furnished that explanation at the time the first book of the Bible was written (or, indeed, at any time), or have given the complementary comment upon it which we have received through the last of the inspired writers. This is not man; it is none other than the Alpha and Omega, the First and the Last, and the Living One, who is and who was, and who is to come (Rev. i.).

But men *love* to be deceived. This is a common trait of humanity; and what can account for this fact but the explanation that the race, in Adam, submitted voluntarily to the influence of the deceiver of the world? This *willingness* to be deceived is strikingly evinced by the readiness with which the natural man gives ear to all who teach the pleasing doctrine that existing conditions are in the main satisfactory, and, anyhow, are steadily improving. We are exhorted to listen to the throb of twentieth century activity and to keep in step with the march of progress. And if this be too materialistic for some, the same vague and meaningless sentiments are put into various religious settings; as in a New Year's greeting to his flock by an eminent divine, the central exhortation was to "bow before the sacred shrine of humanity." Will any reader be surprised to hear that there was a demand for, and a wide distribution of, this greeting? Such phrases as these, whereof every worldling, whether clerical or secular, has a goodly stock, possess an amazing power of *deception,* producing upon the natural mind the effect of intellectual anaesthesia, an effect which cannot be accounted for save by the event recorded in the third of Genesis.

Other evidences of the present working and widespread effects of this power of deception might be multiplied. We see it in the very general love of men for the improbable and unreal, and in the many ways in which human credulity manifests and gratifies itself; in the fondness for fiction, works of the imagination, romances, theatrical representations, so-called spiritualistic seances, feats of legerdemain, tales of occult happenings—in a word, anything and every tiling which represents unreality as reality or which aims to cheat the senses. Falsehood has thus a power even to entertain, to administer gratification, and to divert the mind, though it can never satisfy the heart of man; and when falsehood is presented in attractive forms and with practised skill, it is even exalted as " Art," and to it high religious authorities attribute a beneficial influence; and it even finds its way into the churches.

Not such is the teaching of the Word of God. The man who is controlled thereby finds *his* delight in the law of the Lord. His enjoyment is not in " foolish talking and jesting, which are not convenient"; but he talks of all "His wondrous works " (Ps. cv.). God's words are in his heart; and he talks of them when he sits in his house, and when he walks by the way, and when he lies down, and when he rises up (Deut. vi. 6, 7). Over him the deceiver has no power; for having been enlightened by the "Word of God, he is not ignorant of the deceptive devices of the enemy.

Chapter Thirteen - The Conditions of Faith

THE pursuit by the natural man of first one and then another of the many forms which unreality takes, and the willingness to be deceived, which the man himself recognizes even while he yields to it, are evidences of his lost condition. Until he comes under the convicting work of the Holy Spirit, man will avoid meeting the truth that he has lost fellowship with God. Yet his very willingness to hear of something improbable, and to invest it with attributes of reality, is a perpetual witness to the conscious lack of something which is outside all worldly experiences, which the world knows nothing of, and which the natural man knows nothing of; for " the natural man receiveth not the things of the Spirit of God, for they are foolishness unto him, neither can *he know them*, because they are **spiritually discerned**" (1 Cor. ii. 14),

The readiness of the mind of man to accord to falsehood that acceptance which, in a clear and unfallen mental state, would be accorded only to truth, may be seen in the prevalence throughout the whole world of idolatry, superstition, and false religion. The heathen world, embracing more than two-thirds of the living human beings, is completely under the sway of falseliood and darkness. But the so-called civilized peoples exhibit precisely the same tendencies. Religious, medical, and other quacks flourish in the centres of highest intelligence, and it is safe to say that no man is free from the inherited tendency to give heed and credence to the improbable and untrue.

And when men are not thus occupied, as were the Athenians, who "spent their time in nothing else but either to tell or to hear some new thing," they fall into the mental occupation of " exercising the imagination." Whatever that faculty may have been intended for, its chief exercise in fallen man is to spin long skeins of falsehood, presenting to the mind a succession of unrealities and impossibilities in great variety. The fact that their character is known does not interrupt the process; and like the objective diversions in which men engage to " kill the time " while hastening on to eternity, these imaginations serve to crowd out all profitable subjects of meditation, and to exclude the knowledge of God. Therefore, the Apostle speaks of one phase of the Christian warfare as "casting down imaginations, and every high thing that exalteth itself against the knowledge of God, and bringing every thought into captivity to the obedience of Christ " (2 Cor. x. 5).

There is a spiritual consequence which men bring upon themselves by having "received not the love of the truth "; and that consequence is the subject of our present consideration — namely, that they are always ready " to believe the lie," easily subject to "strong delusion," and exposed to all " signs and lying wonders," and to all " deceivable-ness of unrighteousness " (2 Thess. ii. 9-11).

Such are the effects not only spread plainly in view on every hand, but within the common experiences of every heart; effects of what 1 Is there any explanation, which even purports to account for these effects and to state the cause of them, save only the information given in the third of Genesis?

Chapter Fourteen - Divine Agencies in The World

ALTHOUGH the affairs of the world are at present in the control of Satan and are directed according to his policy; and although the time when the sovereignty of the world shall become the sovereignty of our God and of his Christ is yet in the future (Rev. xi. 15), there are, nevertheless. Divine agencies now acting *in* the world, and acting with almighty power to accomplish God's purpose for this age. Because of the presence of these Divine agencies the world is a very different affair from what it otherwise would be. The presence in it of even a small number of believers who truly have the Spirit and the
testimony of God affects the character of the whole. Moreover, in all the unfoldings of human history, even while man has been permitted freely to choose his own way, God has, nevertheless, been overruling, has been steadily executing the counsels of His own will, and has been making even the
wrath of men to praise Him. We have thus far, and for the sake of the clearer treatment of the subject, made but small reference to these Divine agencies. Let us now briefly consider them and learn what God is accomplishing through them during this present dispensation.

It has pleased God, for reasons which He has not revealed to His creatures, to permit the experiment upon which humanity entered in Eden to be worked out to its present stage, and to give full opportunity for a disclosure of the results of Satan's leadership. It has required many centuries for the working out of this experiment, but in God's sight these have been but as a few days, and when the end is reached He will be justified and every mouth will be stopped (Rom. iii. 19). But God has not abandoned His creature to be destroyed with his own experiment. On the contrary. He has always provided a way to return to Himself. This way has ever been accessible, and has been sought and found by those who have perceived the folly of sin and of continuing the vain attempt to make an abode of comfort and blessing in a Godless world.

During the age in which we live the Divine agencies in this world (which agencies while in it are in direct opposition to its projects, occupations, and diversions, and particularly in opposition to its god and prince) are the Written Word and the Holy Spirit. The Word is given as the basis of faith—to the end that men may believe to the saving of their souls (John xx. 31). The mission of the Holy Spirit is to convince men of the sin of unbelief, of the *righteousness* of Christ, which is freely offered to all, and of the *judgment* of sin which He bore for all who accept Him (John xvi. 8; 1 Cor. i. 30; Rom. viii. 1). In so doing God is not converting the world (Scripture does not promise that such will be the result of preaching the Gospel), but is "' taking out from the nations a people for His name" (Acts xv. 14).

This is the work of God in this age, clearly announced in the inspired Scriptures given at its beginning. Anyone with the most ordinary powers of observation can see for himself this work now going on, and though it be but one here and another there who is seen to turn from " the way of the world" and to seek the only true and " living way," the aggregate is " a great multitude which no man can number."

No explanation save that of Scripture can account for the world. No explanation save that of Scripture can account for the Church of Christ, If men would but apply in this case the same process of reasoning that they employ in other matters, and would accept the conclusions to which that process leads, the Scriptural explanation would, upon these facts alone, be accepted by all thoughtful persons. But the scientific man ceases to be scientific, and the philosopher ceases to be philosophical, and the rationalist ceases to be rational, just when he comes to these matters of highest importance. Here is another remarkable fact; and again we have no explanation of it save that given in Scripture. Why should this be so, were it not that the god of this world succeeds in blinding the minds of the unbelieving lest the light of the Gospel of Christ should dawn upon them? (2 Cor. iv. 4).

This, then, is the doctrine of Scripture—the command which Scripture gives to the believer is to live in the world as one who does not belong to it, as a stranger in it and a pilgrim through it, as a foreigner whose "citizenship is in heaven" (Phil. iii. 20, R.V.).

This command is to be received not merely as a pious sentiment, but as a living and governing principle—" be ye separate." And what else would one wish who recognizes the truth? Truth has ever a sanctifying (*i.e.* separating) effect. The Lord Jesus prays for His followers, saying: "Sanctify them by Thy truth; *Thy Word is* truth" (John xvii. 17). If one believed the truth as declared by Jesus Christ, he would desire, if but as a matter of expediency, to withdraw himself from, and to sever every tie connecting him with, the perishing order of things which is administered by Christ's enemy. How much the more, if he knows, loves, trusts, and waits for the Lord Jesus, will he wish to find no satisfaction, ease, comfort, or pleasure, in a system whose leaders cast Him out and crucified Him, and who would do the same to-day?

Chapter Fifteen – The Way of Deliverance

"Who gave Himself for our sins, that He might deliver us from this present evil age, according to the will of God and our Father" (Gal. i. 4).

THE foregoing picture of the world is one to fill the heart with awe and gloom; and well it might if this were all that Scripture revealed on this subject. "We know now—that is, if we believe the Bible—how this vast organization came into existence, and who is its presiding genius. This information, however, is not all the truth which the Bible discloses concerning this earth, which was created to be man's habitation. It is only the dark story of the past and present. But there is a future. While the world in its present condition is aptly described in Scripture as " this present darkness," we are not left to grope our way through that darkness.

We are, indeed, in "a dark place," but we have a light bright enough to guide us through it. " We have also a more sure word of prophecy; whereunto ye do *well* that ye take heed in your hearts, as unto *a light that shineth in a dark place*" (2 Pet. i. 19). We have, indeed, an enemy who is full of guile; but if we avail ourselves of our Bibles, " we are not ignorant of his devices" (2 Cor. ii. 11).

Unfortunately for the whole world, this light of prophecy, given for the special purpose of guiding us through the present darkness, is sadly neglected by Christians, and we can safely infer to whose influence this neglect is due. The effects of the power of the deceptions that are in the world are not by any means confined to unbelievers. All human beings, so long as they are in " this present evil world," are to some extent under the influence of that power. The spiritually-blind man does not, upon conversion, receive clearness of vision, but is in a perturbed state wherein he " sees men as trees walking." The regenerated soul does not step out of gross darkness directly into the full light of truth. On the contrary, the path of the justified man is rather " as the light of dawn, which shineth *more and more* unto the perfect day" (Prov. iv. 18, R.V., marg.). Hence the general neglect by Christians of the " more sure word of prophecy."

Satan does not lose his interest in a man when he is converted to God. On the contrary, it is after the new nature is given that the conflict begins (Rom. vii.). Not that the regenerated man can ever fall into Satan's hands again, for none of the Good Shepherd's flock shall ever perish, nor shall any be plucked out of His hand (John x. 28); but the influence of the Christian upon the unbelieving world can be limited. Hence it is the desire of Satan to arrange compromises between the believer and tl>e world, and so to occupy the time of the former with the affairs of the latter that he shall exert no influence for the saving of souls, and have no time for the study of the Word. Neglect of the Bible, and *particularly of prophecy*, thus directly serves Satan's purposes; whereas, all Scripture is profitable, and is given by God to the express end that the man of God should be "thoroughly furnished unto all good works" (2 Tim. iii. 16, 17).

Thus it is that, through the influence of the world upon all mankind, and particularly because of the ascendancy which the world has been steadily gaining in the nominal and professing church, the light of prophecy is neglected, and the above-quoted passage is treated as if it read, " we have a very uncertain word of prophecy, to which you do well to pay no attention whatever."

But *God's* people are waking up to the recognition of this neglect, and are beginning to realize the importance of studying that part of the Word which contains yet unfulfilled prophecy. This awakening is, indeed, one of the many and increasingly numerous signs which indicate the near approach of that long-expected time of the restitution of all things which God has spoken by the mouth of *all* His holy prophets since the world began (Acts iii. 21).

We do not here enter upon the great range, extent, and detail of "the more sure word of prophecy." It is enough for our present purposes to say that from

Scripture we may learn that the joint enterprise of man and Devil will speedily be brought to an end; that the end will be destruction; that the debris of the world-system will be swept off the stage and consumed in the fires of judgment; that the powers of heaven shall be shaken, and the inhabitants of earth be terribly afraid; that the same Jesus who from the Mount of Olives ascended into heaven shall so come again in like manner as He went into heaven; that He will banish all sorrow, pain, and fear, and will bring in everlasting righteousness; that nations shall come to His light, and kings to the brightness of His rising; that the government shall be upon His shoulder, and of the increase of His government and peace there shall be no end; that the desert shall rejoice and blossom as the rose; and that the earth shall be full of the knowledge of Jehovah as the waters cover the sea.

Such is the word of prophecy; and it is "sure," because the mouth of Jehovah hath spoken it, who also is faithful and will bring it to pass.

In the power and light of His sure Word of prophecy it is possible, nay, it is easy, to withdraw our affection from the world and from the things that are in the world. In that light we may view with perfect tranquillity the disintegration of all that is connected with this present visible order of things; for though "the world passeth away and the lust thereof," nevertheless we, who believe the Word of God, "look for new heavens and a new earth wherein dwelleth righteousness" (2 Pet. iii. 13).

In glancing backward over the subjects touched upon in these pages the reader will observe that the prominent and universal traits and tendencies of human nature, and the most pronounced characteristics of human society have been traced to, and shown to be fully explained by, the record of the third chapter of Genesis. Rather we may say (inasmuch as Genesis has been aptly termed "the seed-plot of the Bible") that the few words contained in the first seven verses of that chapter are the seeds whereof all true descriptions of the human heart and of human society are the ripened harvest. Whence came words of such immense reach and compass that they give us, in this remote day, the only explanation of the origin of the world-system? From whom could they have come except from Him whose hand places in the tiny seed the germ of the mighty tree?

Chapter Sixteen - The Truth About "Evolution"

IN the foregoing chapters we have taken the collapse of the Darwinian theory of the *origin of species* as a starting point for a fresh examination of the account of the fall of man given in the third chapter of Genesis. It has been pointed out that the facts of human history and human nature, which the Darwinian theory failed utterly to explain, and in presence of which it could not stand as a philosophical theory, are fully and satisfactorily explained by the Genesis narrative.

In pursuing further the inquiry into what gave to the Darwinian hypothesis its ready and wide acceptance among the learned, the writer has been greatly impressed by the fact that there is undoubtedly a sphere within which the process of evolution, as broadly stated by Herbert Spencer, does operate. Certain conclusions follow from this fact, which it is my present purpose to set forth.

The rise and spread of the doctrine of Evolution, in the form given to it by Darwin, Huxley, and Spencer, is one of the striking events of the last half of the nineteenth century. As an explanation of the process whereby every object and thing, animate and inanimate, in all the visible universe came to be what it is, the doctrine of Evolution received well-nigh universal acceptance among the wise and learned of the earth.

It is true that here and there a voice was raised, protesting that the sweeping generalizations of this teaching were wholly unsupported by evidence; but these voices were drowned in the general chorus with which the teaching was acclaimed.

It is likewise true that a few simple souls, uninfluenced even by scepticism displayed and taught in the pulpit, clung to the narrative of creation given in the first chapter of Genesis. But those who refused to accept the new teaching were in the main hopelessly "unscientific" and "behind the times."

In that first chapter of Genesis, containing only 31 verses, the Author quietly states nine times over (a three-fold emphasis multiplied by three) that living creatures were commanded to reproduce each "*after his kind.*" This remarkable but unobtrusive iteration seems now like a challenge to the evolutionist, and to indicate a prevision of a time to come in the old age of the world when a doctrine should be put forth and should be accepted by all whose faith was not firmly anchored in the accuracy of Scripture, according to which doctrine every living thing is a link in a long chain connecting it with ancestry of *another kind,* and according to which every living thing has the tendency to produce offspring of *another kind* than its own.

We say that the spread of this doctrine of Evolution was a remarkable phenomenon: the astonishing feature of it being that there has never been produced in support of it so much as a *single instance* of the reproduction by one living thing of offspring of a different species; and that there never has been produced a single fact tending in the slightest degree to prove that such a thing ever happened anywhere in the universe.

In view of this state of the evidence, how is the almost universal acceptance of Darwin's theory of the Origin of Species, and particularly the theory of the descent of man, to be accounted for? Its wide acceptance is unquestionably a *fact,* and hence is susceptible of an explanation.

One reason for the rapid spread of the doctrine undoubtedly is that it afforded a platform from which the unbeliever could, in the name of science, contradict the Bible account of creation, and thus discredit the Bible as a whole. Haeckel very aptly termed Darwin's *Origin of Species* an " Anti-Genesis," saying: " With a single stroke Darwin has annihilated the dogma of creation." We know in a general way how it has fared since that time with Genesis. How has it fared with the " Anti-Genesis?"

The unregenerate man, whether a professing Christian or not, is always seeking to justify his unbelief. Hence the ready acceptance of Darwin's theory.

But there is a more profound reason than this for the fact we are seeking to explain, and our present object is to set forth this deeper reason.

Chapter Seventeen - Two Methods of World-Making

MAN has observed in the world and has become acquainted with *two distinct methods of working.* These two methods proceed respectively from different spiritual sources, and are radically different one from the other. One is a method of *evolution* —that is, a method of continual change from one set of conditions to another, with increasing diversity and ramifications, in the effort to work out some far-off result which is not clearly defined to consciousness, and which constantly eludes pursuit. The other is a method of *creation,* according to which the plan and pattern of each thing is complete and perfect from the beginning, admitting of no improvement or development. One method is that of a mighty but imperfect spiritual being, who aims at attaining, after a long succession of failures, some ideal state or result, and who in that endeavour perseveringly evolves one new expedient after another, as successive failures materialize. The other method is that of an Omnipotent and All-wise Being, who works after the counsel of His own perfect will, who has no need to experiment, and with whom failure is impossible. One method is that of Satan; the other method is that of Jehovah-Elohim.

The universe was created by the word of God. " By the word of the Lord were the heavens made, and all the host of them by the breath of His mouth " (Ps. xxxiii. 6). The earth too was formed by His word, and filled with living things, vegetable and animal, each of which was bidden to bring forth "*after his kind.*" Each of His creatures has fulfilled this command; and in all the earth there is not an instance wherein a living thing has brought forth seed which was not " after his kind." The earth itself could not contain the figures which would represent the acts of reproduction that have taken place in it, but among them all there is not known a single departure from this command. This is the method of Creation—God's method; and all talk of differentiation, and integration, and progression from the homogeneous to the heterogeneous, of primal nebulosity and primordial protoplasm, and all the rest of it, has no more solid foundation than *Gulliver's Travels*.

The method of *evolution* is found *only in human affairs and nowhere else in the universe.* This method—namely, that of getting one's eyes opened and becoming as gods, knowing good and evil, and thus being able to discern and discriminate, to choose and experiment and fail, and choose again— was proposed by its author to the first parents of the human race, and was adopted by them. The words are recorded for us: "Certainly ye shall not die; for God doth know that in the day ye eat thereof, then your eyes shall be opened, and ye shall be as gods, knowing good and evil." Adam thus committed the human race to the method of evolution, and the affairs of humanity have proceeded according to that method ever since.

The mistake that the philosophers of materialism have made is just this: Having traced out a law or method of development or progress in all human affairs and institutions, and^ being unilluminated by the Word of truth, because they rejected it, they have hastily and eagerly accepted the conclusion that evolution is an universal method. Unbelieving theologians in turn (which our seminaries turn out by the hundreds), fearful of being thought " unscientific " and " not abreast of modern thought," have accepted evolution as God's method of creation; and thus the whole world has wondered after the beast. And now the grim humour of the situation is evident to those who have eyes to see and wit to appreciate it, in that the doctrine of *evolution itself* is becoming a mere phase in the *evolution of philosophy*, and is taking its place in the prodigious mass of junk and debris which "Evolution" has left in its wake. " He that sitteth in the heavens shall laugh: the Lord shall have them in derision."

We may be sure that Satan desires that his method should be well thought of, whatever he may now—after these centuries of testing—think of it himself; and doubtless he takes much satisfaction in having imposed upon apostate Christendom the belief that his method of evolution was the Divine method of creation.

Chapter Eighteen - No Evolution Outside Human Affairs

THE matter under consideration is of sufficient importance to justify a closer examination of it. Of the lack of any trace of the operation of evolution outside of human affairs, but little need be said. It has been frequently pointed out that, if evolution were a law of nature it would be in operation in our day, and the earth would be full of the evidences of its working. But so far from the existence of a single scrap of evidence for such a law (outside of human affairs), the effort to cross the line of species by artificial means has totally failed. Even so stout an advocate of evolution as Prof. Huxley was forced, before his death, to admit that " The present state of knowledge furnishes us with no link between the living and the not-living." And Tyndall said: " Every attempt made in our day to generate life independent of antecedent life has utterly broken down."

Furthermore, if created things had come into their present forms by a process of evolution from primal nebulae and primordial protoplasm, the crust of the earth would be full of, and the surface of the earth would be strewn with, innumerable *intermediate forms* filling the gaps between the species, and showing historically the progress from one species to another. Instead of this there has not been found, in all these years of search, so much as a single specimen of an intermediate form.

In Rev. J. Urquhart's *The Bible, and How to read it*, Vol. II., chap, iii., entitled "Darwinism and Genesis," there is given a very luminous description of the four fundamental assumptions of the Darwinian theory, each one of which is essential to its support. The author further shows very conclusively, and largely by reference to the published conclusions of sceptical men of science, that each one of these assumptions has utterly failed for lack of support. Finally he presents unanswerable facts and considerations which oppose the Darwinian theory. "We quote the concluding paragraphs:

"Much more might be added; but the overthrow of the foundations on which Darwinism is confessedly built makes it impossible for this theory to maintain its hold upon science. If any further proof of its erroneousness were required, it would be found in the story told by the fossils. If animals had been *evolved,* we should have found the strata occupied at first by animal remains of *one form only*. Then by-and-by we should have seen these diverge from each other by small variations. The differences would then become more marked, until perfectly distinct forms were reached. We certainly would not expect to encounter at the very outset numerous forms which were entirely different, which were fully developed, and which did not afterwards vary, but continued in every respect the same, age after age. We should not, I repeat, expect to discover this; for such radical distinction of the forms and the absence of change in them afterwards would alike be fatal to the theory. *But this is what we do find.* There are wide differences in the forms from the very first, and *some of the earliest* continue to the present hour unchanged. When new forms enter, their entrance has not been preceded by variations of earlier life which lead us to look for the coming of these. ' The new forms,' says the late Duke of Argyll, [1] 'always appear *suddenly*' — from no known source—and generally if of a new type, exhibiting that type in great strength as to numbers and in great perfection as regards organization. The usual way of evading this great difficulty in the facts of Geology is to plead what is called the imperfection of the Record. But this plea will not avail us here. There are some tracks of time regarding which our records are as complete as we could desire. In the Jurassic rocks we have a continuous and undisturbed series of long and tranquil deposits—containing a complete record of all the new forms of life which were introduced during these ages of oceanic life. And those ages were, as a fact, long enough to see not only a thick (1300 feet) mass of deposit, but the first appearance of hundreds of new species. These are all as definite and distinct from each other as existing species. No less than 1850 new species have been counted—all of them suddenly born—all of them lasting only for a time, and all of them in their turn superseded by still newer forms. There is no sign of mixture, or of confusion, or of infinitesimal or of indeterminate variations. These " Medals of Creation " are all, each of them, struck by a *new die*, which never failed to impress itself on the plastic materials of this truly *creative* work. There is nothing more instructive than to place a series of these new species, such as the Ammonites, side by side. The perfect regularity and beauty of each new pattern of shell, and the fixity of it so long as it lasted at all, are features as striking as they are obvious.'

"In the face of such facts, it is astonishing that Darwinism could ever have found acceptance. But, after all, it is not more astonishing than many another belief that has been the fashion or the idol of an hour. Man's word changes and disappears. 'The Word of the Lord endureth for ever.'"

[1] *Organic Evolution Cross-Examined, pp. 145-147.*

Chapter Nineteen - Evolution Universal in Human Affairs

So much for the proposition that no trace of evolution is found outside of human affairs. We now turn to the other proposition— namely, that evolution *is* the method of procedure which obtains in all human affairs. If this proposition be as clear as the first, the two facts viewed together present a very startling condition of things, and one which wonderfully confirms the truth and accuracy of the first seven verses of the third chapter of Genesis.

The fact that evolution is the method which obtains in human affairs, and has marked, by its workings, the history of the race everywhere and in all time, is very easily shown. The exceptions, which strikingly confirm the rule, are where God Almighty intervenes and acts in human affairs directly and according to His own method. There is no evolution in the Bible, the Word of God, which was "for ever settled in heaven," and which remains unchanged and unchangeable. There is no evolution in the miracles of the Lord Jesus Christ. There is no evolution when a soul is regenerated and becomes a new creature in Christ (2 Cor. V. 17). In all these instances the plan and pattern of the creation is complete and perfect from the beginning. [1]

A few illustrations of the operation of evolution in human affairs will enable the reader to see for himself its universality.

In society at large we find a broad illustration. This is one of the illustrations employed by Herbert Spencer. He says (*First Principles*, chap, xiv. sec. 3): "In the social organism integrative changes are clearly and abundantly exemplified." And so they are; and it was upon clear and abundant illustrations drawn from this fertile source that his entire " law of evolution," with all its pomposity and ponderosity, was founded. Influenced by evidences from the realm where evolution *does* live and rule, author and readers alike were easily persuaded to assign to it a like existence and rule in realms where *no trace of it has ever been found*. Spencer goes on to cite the development of society through wandering families, then tribes, then stronger tribes formed by the conjunction or subjugation of weaker ones, until the combinations, after being repeatedly formed and broken up, become relatively permanent, and ultimately evolve into states and nationalities. That process, as the result of which, after many changes, nations have been aggregated, is "evolution." In that process, as Mr Spencer notes and points out, there are three kinds of changes, which proceed with practical regularity and continuity: *first,* a change from a less coherent to a more coherent state; *second,* a change from a more homogeneous to a less homogeneous state; and *third,* a change from a less definite to a more definite state. The. presence of these characteristic marks are everywhere and during all historic times manifested in human affairs, and they hence furnish very strong evidence of the existence of an invisible presiding genius who, from generation to generation, continues to direct the progress of humanity.

[1] It seems hardly necessary to remind the reader of the difference between evolution and growth (which may characterize a creature). Evolution is the development of a thing or set of things into something else. Growth is the development of an organism into itself; i.e. its maturity; first the blade, then the ear, then the full corn in the ear.

Chapter Twenty - No Evolution Among the Lower Animals

THE absence of these marks in every other part of the accessible universe also tends to indicate that the sway of this invisible presiding genius is strictly limited to the affairs of men. It is a very striking fact that there is no evolution in the affairs of other living creatures. For example, and in marked contrast with the evolution of *human* society, such animals as herd together have developed *no changes whatever* in the way the herds are formed. The birds build their nests, and the affairs of the ant-colonies and beehives are conducted *precisely* as they have always been conducted since men began to observe them.

We need have no doubt at all as to our conclusions thus far. Evolution is an undeniable fact in human affairs; and we can see that it continues to operate in our day precisely as it has operated in the past. Thus we have the important fact that, in the sphere where evolution does actually operate, it has continued to operate. By this fact we have a sure answer to the question which has puzzled evolutionists—namely, Why does organic evolution no longer act in altering the structures of plants and animals, and in other spheres where no trace of its action is now seen? If it ever did so act, surely it should have continued so to do. The answer is that evolution never operated in those spheres, else it would be operating there still; and that all things in those spheres came into existence in some other way than by the operation of the process of evolution.

Another inference which may be drawn at this point is that the affairs of the human race have in some way come under the sway of a ruler, or at least of an impersonal law, who or which does *not exercise control* over other orders of creation. These humbler orders of living beings perform perfectly, and without experiment or mistake, all the operations needful for their existence and well-being, and for the perpetuation of their species, some of which operations are extremely complex and require for their performance a high degree of technical skill, Man alone blunders in everything that he undertakes. And the difference is just this, that *man has departed from God's plan, while the other created orders have not.*

Chapter Twenty-One - Effects of Evolution

BUT evolution is seen at work not merely in forming social organizations as a whole, but in giving ever new and different shapes to the sub-divisions of the social mass; as if ever striving after an ideal and ever failing of its realization. Thus, evolution is seen in operation when we examine the history of all social subclasses, such as the industrial groups, the ecclesiastical, the military, the medical, the legal, the artistic, scientific, etc.

Take, for instance, in the industrial class, the method of cultivating the ground. Not so many centuries ago the rudest kind of an implement served the purpose of ploughing the soil, while the gathering of crops and threshing of grain were carried on by hand in the most primitive fashion. By successive and almost imperceptible stages men have evolved classes of exceedingly complex machines, whereby ploughing, seeding, reaping, binding, threshing, etc., are performed automatically and with a minimum of human intervention and oversight. In this "evolution" each new member of the long series has made its way *by the destruction of what went before*, a characteristic of evolution being that it leaves in its wake a constantly accumulating mass of debris composed of obsolete links in the series.

If we look along other industrial lines, such as milling, locomotion, printing, paper-making, spinning and weaving, communicating intelligence to distant points, etc., etc., we see precisely the same kinds of changes going on from incoherence and homogeneity to coherence and heterogeneity, accompanied by the destruction of forms existing at previous stages.

These illustrations from the industrial world are most impressive, because, in that sphere, evolution is most active at present; but wherever we look in the realm of human affairs the evidences of evolution are seen in the greatest abundance; whereas the moment we pass the line of human affairs we strain our eyes in vain for a scrap of evidence to show that the process of evolution ever had a foothold.

In the literary field, for example, we can readily trace the literary activity of man from its simple beginnings in oral recitation and manuscript copies to the manifold present-day output of books, newspapers, and periodicals in infinite variety.

Pictorial art has had a like development from crude outline drawing to the many different forms and methods of picture-making which are in vogue to-day.

Likewise in sciences, such as chemistry, and in the practice of medicine, an evolution is constantly going on, of precisely the same sort as exemplified by the above illustrations, involving integration and differentiation, and constantly erecting each new set of conditions upon the ruins of the old.

Or to look in quite another direction, we may see in the man-made religions of the world the same sort of development, from the simple beginning made by Adam's eldest son, in presenting to God the results of his own efforts and rejecting God's way of salvation by vicarious sacrifice, to the manifold and complex religious systems of the present day, all of which are mere ramifications or evolutions of the original principle adopted by Cain—namely, that man can do something to save himself, or to render himself acceptable to God. The only religion which, in all man's history, has not varied, is that based upon the atoning blood, and which recognizes that man can do nothing for himself, but is shut up to the grace of God; for— " By *faith* Abel offered unto God a more excellent sacrifice than Cain, by which he obtained witness that he was righteous, God testifying of his gifts; and by it he being dead yet speaketh" (Heb. xi. 4).

The reader may push this investigation as far as he likes, and will find everywhere in human affairs, and *nowhere else,* the evidences of the operation of the law of evolution from the moment Adam and Eve applied their newly-acquired power of discrimination and their thirst for progress to the invention of aprons, down to the present moment, without interruption.

In the sphere of human affairs the evidences of this process are copious and even superabundant, insomuch that a lifetime would not suffice to examine them all. Outside that sphere they are non-existent. Has this remarkable fact no lesson for the unbelieving reader? Genesis iii. 1-7 contains an explanation of this fact. Can any other be brought forward?

Chapter Twenty-Two - The Error of The Evolutionist

IT is very interesting to note how Mr Spencer uses his data, and how he joins the illustrations taken by him from human affairs to those taken from other spheres. When he speaks of evolution in human society, whether the development of nations, or of industries, or of arts, or fashions, or ecclesiastical systems, his facts are drawn either from history or from matters of everyday observation. Having verified his proposition by apt and copious illustrations drawn from these sources, the unwary reader is apt not to notice that, when our philosopher goes beyond the sphere of human affairs, he has not a *single verified fact* to adduce—everything is either conjecture or assumption. For example, he speaks of the Sidereal System as having evolved from a nebulous state to its present condition; of the evolution of the earth from a mass of molten matter to its present condition; of the evolution of living organisms from primordial protoplasm to the present highly differentiated organisms, including man. In all this there is not one fact, not a scintilla of evidence, to warrant the assumptions presented. On the contrary, and as shown in the first part of this article, all these assumptions utterly fail of support; and the evidence to the contrary puts them wholly out of court.

Having arrived at Man, the character of the illustrations given by Mr Spencer changes at once, from fiction and fancy, to undeniable fact, showing, what we affirm to be the case, that up to the appearance of man upon the earth, about six thousand years ago (there is absolutely no evidence for an earlier date), evolution had no part at all in fashioning the earth or the creatures in and upon it; and neither since that time has evolution had any part in fashioning the earth or its inhabitants; but, on the other hand, that in all which man has set himself to do and accomplish in self-will, or in accordance with the will of another, not that of God Himself, evolution has been the invariable and universal method of procedure. Evolution is undeniably the order of this present world wherein evil is found (for *evil*, like evolution, is *not found outside of man's world*), and there is no escape from it for sinful man except by death. Therefore Christ " gave Himself for our sins that He *might deliver us from this present evil world,* according to the will of God and our Father " (Gal. i. 4).

Chapter Twenty-Three - Degeneration

ONE common quality of all the products of evolution, which serves to distinguish them from all the products of creation, is the *instability* of the former, and their tendency to revert to their original condition, that is, to the condition into which they were brought by *creation*. This ineradicable tendency to progress *backwards* has been a sore trial to evolutionists. They had to take note of a fact so patent and universal, and room had, therefore, to be made in the evolutionary scheme for " dissolution " and " reversion to type "; and having thus provided sonorous names for these phenomena, our philosophers had therewith to be content. But has any evolutionist, or anyone else, ever produced a single instance of reversion to type in the spheres of *creation?* Again we have a very striking confirmation of our main proposition. In all the types as God created them there is neither evolution nor reversion. The types neither advance nor recede. Reversion to type occurs only where evolution has come in, and it proceeds just so far as to obliterate man's treatment of God's material. Having proceeded so far, it stops just there. In a word, reversion, when not interfered with, *simply undoes what evolution has done.*

It is as if each type was held to its place by an elastic cord. Man can pull it in various directions, thus producing "varieties" of plants and animals; but never can he stretch it far enough to cross the line of species. "After his kind" is the inflexible law of reproduction. And when man has relaxed his pressure on the type, the elastic cord quickly draws it back to its primal condition, and the effect of man's operations is obliterated. This is " reversion to type."

Hence all the speculation which pictures the return of the cosmos to its conjectured gaseous state, to begin evoluting all over again, is the wildest kind of unfounded nonsense. To such fancies as these do men—the wisest and best of them—expose themselves, when they reject the Word of God, with its simple, sufficient, and satisfactory account of creation, and of the entrance of evil and death upon a scene which God prepared for His own glory in the happiness of His creatures. It is a fearful thing not to receive a love of the truth. All who are thus deluded, and who thus reject the truth in order to follow their own vain imaginations into realms where the natural man cannot penetrate, are given over to a strong delusion that they should believe *the lie,* "because they receive not the love of *the truth,* that they might be saved" (2 Thess. ii. 10, 11).

If it be true that evolution appertains solely to the conduct of the affairs of man in his fallen state, that evolution is the plan of progress adopted by man after his departure from God, we see what an affront has been offered to the Creator, the Son of God, by whom "were all things created that are in heaven and that are on earth, visible and invisible" (Col. i. 16), in attributing to Him the method of His enemy. But such has been man's way from the beginning. God put man in the garden to dress and keep it, and to have dominion over all creation; but he preferred Satan's plan of becoming as god by the pursuit of Knowledge. God offered men again the Prince of Life, but they chose a murderer. This was the significance of the choice presented by Pilate, and as the Apostle Peter subsequently declared (Acts iii. 14): "But ye denied the Holy One and the Just, and desired a *murderer* to be granted unto you; and killed the Prince of Life." They preferred the devil, and " he was a murderer from the beginning" (John viii. 44). God sent the True Light into the world, and men preferred the prince of darkness. "And this is the condemnation, that light is come into the world, and that men loved darkness rather than light, because their deeds were evil" (John iii. 19). God sent the truth in the person of His Son (John i. 17, xiv. 6, xviii. 37); but men preferred the devil, who " abode not in the truth, because there is no truth in him; ... for he is a liar and the father of it" (John viii. 44).

It is not strange then, that when this pursuit of Knowledge had reached its limit of folly and madness, the works and workings of the devil should be attributed to Him who was manifested for the express purpose of destroying them. " For this purpose the Son of God was manifested, that He might destroy the works of the devil" (1 John iii. 8).

Chapter Twenty-Four - Conclusion

WE find, then, that changes of the kind which philosophers call " evolutionary " are the invariable incident of *all* human institutions; and on the other hand that evolutionary changes occur nowhere else in the known universe. It may be said that there is *nothing* which so peculiarly characterizes human affairs, and so clearly distinguishes them from all other parts of the universe, as the fact that the former are subject without interruption to evolutionary changes, from which all other parts of creation are exempt.

This is a fact of truly immense significance; and what explanation can be given of a difference so extraordinary and so profound? What adequate explanation can there be if we reject that which the Scriptures supply—namely, that human affairs, since the fall of the parents of the race, have not been conducted according to God's plan and method, but according to the plan and method of another? Evolutionary changes began with man's departure from the plan of God, and have characterized all he has done in his state of departure. They will cease when man's experiment in self-development and self-will shall have been brought to the end towards which it is hastening, and when God's will is done in earth as it is in heaven.

We ask now an answer to our question:

Is the account which we read in the third of Genesis true? If it were merely a matter of finding an hypothesis capable of standing awhile in the niche from which the Darwinian theory has been displaced, the question would not be worth the asking. Neither is it a matter of much consequence whether or not "the thought and culture of the age" adopt a " theistic explanation" of the universe. To defend one theory or to attack another is not an object to which the writer would give any thought or attention. These pages are not written with the object of gaining the reader's acceptance of a theory which may serve as a provisional resting-place for his mental speculations; but "these are written that ye may believe that Jesus is the Christ, the Son of God, and that believing, ye may have…

Life through His Name."

CPSIA information can be obtained
at www.ICGtesting.com
Printed in the USA
BVHW041054230820
587093BV00014B/369